CPC

EXAM STUDY GUIDE

2023-2024

Learn & Excel! Includes Tests | Q&A | Medical Billing and Coding | Terminology | Extra Content

---

Rory George

TABLE OF CONTENTS

Introduction and overview

Welcome to the CPC Test Prep Exam Preparation 2023, your ultimate guide to conquering the Certified Professional Coder (CPC) examination! This comprehensive resource is designed to support your journey toward achieving a successful outcome on this important milestone in your career. With the healthcare industry rapidly evolving, the need for skilled and knowledgeable medical coders has never been more crucial. By obtaining your CPC certification, you will validate your expertise in the field and open doors to an array of exciting professional opportunities.

The book is organized into multiple sections and chapters, each covering a specific area of medical coding, such as terminology, anatomy, ICD-10-CM, CPT, and HCPCS Level II.
In addition, we provide tips and strategies for efficient studying, time management, and reducing test anxiety.
Throughout the guide, you will find practice questions, case studies, and real-world examples to help reinforce the concepts you learn.

As you work through this manual, remember that you must learn more than only rote memorization of numbers and information to pass the CPC exam.

Instead, medical coding principles should be taught based on solid foundations and applied successfully in various clinical settings. We want to help you achieve success on this challenging exam by providing you with the information, skills, and confidence you need.

In the increasingly evolving healthcare industry, a medical coder is essential to precise and efficient communication between medical experts, insurance companies, and patients. Once you are a Certified Professional Coder, you will join a network of professionals dedicated to quality and honesty. The CPC preparation process might be complicated, but you can pass if you stick with it.

As we embark on this educational journey, let's first delve into a detailed overview and description of the Certified Professional Coder (CPC) certification. This prestigious credential, awarded by the American Academy of Professional Coders (AAPC), demonstrates a coder's medical coding knowledge and proficiency in applying that knowledge to real-world scenarios. In this chapter, we'll explore the significance of this certification, the skills and expertise required to obtain it, and the impact it can have on your career in the healthcare industry.

Importance of CPC Certification

In today's competitive job market, having a CPC certification sets you apart from other medical coders. Employers seek candidates who have demonstrated their commitment to excellence and are well-versed in the latest coding practices. By obtaining your CPC certification, you'll validate your expertise in the field and position yourself as a knowledgeable professional in the eyes of potential employers.

Moreover, CPC-certified coders often enjoy higher earning potential than their non-certified counterparts. According to AAPC's annual salary survey, certified coders earn, on average, 20% more than those without certification. This can translate into significantly increasing your earning potential throughout your career.

Skills and Expertise Required

Becoming a CPC requires a solid foundation in medical coding principles and the ability to apply them effectively in various clinical scenarios. Here are some essential skills and areas of expertise that you'll need to master to obtain your CPC certification:

- **Medical Terminology:** To comprehend and code medical records correctly, one must have a solid grasp of medical jargon. This involves understanding word roots, prefixes, and suffixes and identifying regularly used abbreviations and acronyms in medical paperwork.

- **Anatomy and Physiology:** The assignment of appropriate codes to diagnoses and treatments depends on having a thorough understanding of human anatomy and physiology. You'll need to be knowledgeable about the anatomy, physiology, and many systems and organs of the human body.

- **ICD-10-CM:** The primary classification system used to categorize illnesses in the US is called ICD-10-CM, or International Classification of Diseases, Tenth Revision, and Clinical Modification. You must understand the ICD-10-CM system's structure, norms, and rules and be able to assign codes based on the available documentation appropriately.

- **CPT:** A standardized coding system called Current Procedural Terminology (CPT) describes medical operations and services. To become a CPC, you must be an expert user of CPT codes, including their format, rules, and modifiers.

- **HCPCS Level II:** The Healthcare Common Procedure Coding System (HCPCS) Level II is utilized in conjunction with CPT codes to record extra services, supplies, and equipment that CPT does not cover. The structure and rules of HCPCS Level II codes and when to use them must be understood by CPCs.

- **Coding Guidelines and Compliance:** To guarantee accurate, compliant coding practices, it is crucial to have a firm grasp of coding rules and regulations and the significance of following them.

- **Ethical and Legal Considerations:** Being a CPC requires knowing the ethical and legal issues that affect medical coding, such as HIPAA, patient privacy laws, and confidentiality agreements.

Impact on Your Career

Achieving your CPC certification can have a transformative effect on your career in the healthcare industry. Here are some ways that becoming a CPC can benefit your professional development:

- **Enhanced Job Opportunities:** With a CPC certification, you'll be better positioned to secure rewarding job opportunities in various healthcare settings, such as hospitals, physician's offices, outpatient facilities, and insurance companies. Employers recognize the value of certified coders and often prioritize them during hiring.

- **Increased Earning Potential:** As mentioned earlier, CPC-certified coders typically enjoy higher salaries than their non-certified counterparts. This certification can significantly boost your earning potential throughout your career, giving you the financial stability and growth you desire.

- **Professional Recognition:** Earning your CPC certification demonstrates your dedication to excellence and ongoing professional development. This distinction can lead to greater recognition within the industry, opening doors to networking opportunities, promotions, and other career advancements.

- **Continuing Education:** As a CPC, you'll be required to maintain your certification by participating in continuing education and staying current with industry trends and changes. This commitment to lifelong learning will help ensure that you remain at the forefront of your field, further solidifying your value to employers and colleagues.

Preparing for the CPC Exam

Now that you know the CPC certification's significance and effects, you can begin preparing for the exam. The challenging CPC exam contains 100 questions and covers many subjects, including medical terminology, anatomy, ICD-10-CM, CPT, HCPCS Level II, and more. If you want to pass the exam, you must create a strategic study plan that combines academic understanding with real-world application.

We'll go deeper into each subject in the subsequent chapters of this manual, giving you the knowledge, instruments, and resources you need to understand the subject matter and successfully pass the CPC test. To assist you in maximizing your preparation and achieving your best performance on test day, we'll also discuss ideas and tactics for efficient studying, time management, and test-taking approaches.

Remember that learning facts and statistics is only one way to succeed on the CPC test as you move through this guide and your study. Instead, it's about developing a solid understanding of medical coding concepts and using them successfully in various clinical settings. You are well on your way to obtaining your CPC certification and unleashing the full potential of your career in the healthcare field with commitment, dedication, and the assistance of this thorough resource.

CPC Certification Requirements

Before diving into the specifics of the CPC exam, it's essential to understand the requirements for obtaining the CPC certification. The American Academy of Professional Coders (AAPC) has established criteria that candidates must meet to be eligible for the certification. In this section, we'll outline these requirements, helping you ensure that you're on the right track in pursuing this prestigious credential.

Education and Experience

While there is no formal education requirement for the CPC exam, it's strongly recommended that candidates have a high school diploma or equivalent. Additionally, the AAPC suggests that candidates have some background in medical coding or a related field through formal education or work experience.

Although not mandatory, completing a medical coding training program accredited by the AAPC can be highly beneficial in preparing for the CPC exam. These programs cover essential topics such as medical terminology, anatomy, ICD-10-CM, CPT, and HCPCS Level II, providing you with the foundational knowledge necessary for success on the exam.

In terms of experience, the AAPC requires candidates to have a minimum of two years of on-the-job coding experience to obtain the full CPC certification. However, candidates without this experience can still take the exam and earn the CPC-A (Certified Professional Coder-Apprentice) designation.

The CPC-A credential indicates that the candidate has passed the exam but must meet the experience requirement. To remove the "Apprentice" designation and obtain the full CPC certification, candidates must complete the necessary work experience and submit proof to the AAPC.

AAPC Membership

To be eligible to take the CPC exam, candidates must be current members of the AAPC. Membership provides access to valuable resources, networking opportunities, and continuing education, which can enhance your career development and help you stay up-to-date on industry trends and changes.

Exam Registration and Fees

To register for the CPC exam, candidates must complete the online registration through the AAPC's website. You'll be asked to select an exam location, date, and time during registration. Registering early is essential, as seating is limited, and exam slots can fill quickly.

As of the time of writing, the CPC exam fee is $399 for AAPC members. This fee covers the cost of the exam and one free retake if needed. It's important to note that prices are subject to change, so check the AAPC's website for the most up-to-date pricing information.

Exam Preparation

Given the comprehensive nature of the CPC exam, thorough preparation is critical for success. As previously mentioned, completing an accredited medical coding training program can be an invaluable resource in your studies. Additionally, this guide provides the information, tools, and strategies necessary to master the material and confidently tackle the CPC exam.

In conclusion, obtaining your CPC certification requires education, experience, AAPC membership, exam registration, and thorough preparation. By understanding and meeting these requirements, you'll be well on your way to earning this prestigious credential and unlocking the full potential of your career in the healthcare industry. In the subsequent chapters of this guide, we'll dive deeper into the essential topics and strategies for exam success, ensuring that you're fully equipped to take on the challenge of the CPC exam and come out victorious.

CPC Exam Questions: Structure, Content, and Tips

As you prepare for the CPC exam, you must familiarize yourself with the types of questions you'll encounter, the content they cover, and strategies for answering them effectively. In this section, we'll provide an overview of the CPC exam questions, discussing their structure, the topics they address, and tips for confidently tackling them.

Structure of CPC Exam Questions

The CPC exam consists of 100 multiple-choice questions. You'll have 4 hours to complete the exam, so managing your time wisely is crucial. The questions assess your knowledge of medical coding principles and ability to apply them in various clinical scenarios.

Most questions on the CPC exam present a coding case or scenario, followed by four possible answer choices. The answer choices may include code combinations or variations, and your task is to select the most accurate and appropriate option based on the information provided.

Content Covered in CPC Exam Questions

The CPC exam questions cover a wide range of topics related to medical coding, including:

- **Medical Terminologies:** Questions in this category evaluate your comprehension of medical terminology, including root words, prefixes, and suffixes, and your capacity to decipher acronyms and abbreviations used in medical documents.

- **Anatomy and Physiology:** These questions assess your knowledge of human anatomy and physiology, including the structure and function of various body systems and organs.

- **ICD-10-CM:** To correctly assign diagnosis codes based on the available documentation, you must use your understanding of the ICD-10-CM coding system to the questions in this category.

- **CPT:** For this category, you'll need to assign the proper procedure codes using your knowledge of the CPT coding system while considering the system's structure, rules, and modifiers.

- **HCPCS Level II:** Questions about HCPCS Level II codes test your ability to use this additional coding system in conjunction with CPT codes to report extra services, supplies, and equipment not covered by CPT.

- **Coding Guidelines and Compliance:** These inquiries test your knowledge of coding rules and regulations and your awareness of how crucial it is to follow them to ensure accurate coding practices.

- **Ethical and Legal Considerations:** The questions in this category discuss the moral and legal ramifications of medical codings, such as patient confidentiality, privacy, and HIPAA laws.

Tips for Tackling CPC Exam Questions

The following advice will help you answer questions with confidence as you take the CPC exam:

- Before selecting your answer, carefully read the entire question and all possible answers. Pay great attention to the small print and scan it for words or phrases that can hint at the solution.

- As you read through the response options, try to weed out any that are inaccurate or inconsistent with the knowledge that has been given. You can reduce your possibilities and improve your chances of choosing the correct response by using the process of elimination.

- You are permitted to bring your ICD-10-CM, CPT, HCPCS Level II codebooks, and an authorized medical dictionary to the exam. You will need to use these resources to discover the correct codes and validate your answers, so make sure you are familiar with them and know how to use them effectively.

- With 100 questions and 4 hours to complete them, you must pace yourself to complete the exam. Keep an eye on your performance as the test progresses, and try to spend two to three minutes on each question. A complicated question is best handled by making an educated guess rather than spending much time on it. If you run out of time, you can always return to it.

● Taking practice exams and answering sample questions will help you understand the format and content of CPC exam questions. By taking tests, you can assess your knowledge of the subject, improve your test-taking skills, and gain confidence.

● Feel free to test your knowledge and intuition whenever a challenging question arises. When you have prepared and studied well, you are more likely to choose the correct response based on your understanding of the content. Choosing to err on caution over not providing an answer is always a better option.

● Try to remain calm and concentrated during the exam: You will feel anxious during the exam, but keep your composure. You can pass the test after studying effectively if you breathe deeply, have a cheerful attitude, and have a positive outlook. Maintaining focus and managing your time can help you succeed.

● The key to success on the exam is understanding the structure, subject matter, and approaches to the exam questions. By familiarizing yourself with the types of questions you'll encounter and practicing efficient test-taking techniques, you can handle the exam comfortably and prove your medical coding competency. Having faith in your abilities and expertise will help you achieve your goal of becoming a Certified Professional Coder as you proceed with your study and progress through this manual.

CPC Exam Preparation and Information

Proper preparation is critical to success on the CPC exam. In this section, we'll discuss strategies and resources to help you effectively prepare for the exam and essential information to remember before and during the test.

Study Strategies

● **Create a study plan:** Develop a structured study plan that outlines the topics you need to cover and allocates time for reviewing each area. Break down the material into manageable chunks and set milestones to track your progress. Be sure also to schedule time for regular practice exams and review sessions.

● **Use various resources:** Supplement your studies with a range of resources, including this guide, coding manuals, online courses, and textbooks. The more diverse your study materials, the better your understanding of the subject matter will be.

● **Join a study group:** Participating in a study group can be a valuable way to exchange knowledge, ask questions, and discuss challenging topics with fellow exam candidates. You can find study groups through local AAPC chapters or online forums.

● **Focus on practical application:** The CPC exam tests your theoretical knowledge and ability to apply coding principles in real-life scenarios. Practice coding real medical cases and pay attention to the context in which codes are used.

Exam Day Information

- **What to bring:** On exam day, get your ICD-10-CM, CPT, and HCPCS Level II codebooks, an approved medical dictionary, a valid government-issued photo ID, and AAPC member ID. Remember to pack a non-programmable calculator, pencils, and an eraser. All coding manuals must be in print format, and you may not use any electronic devices during the exam.

- **What to wear:** Dress comfortably and in layers to accommodate varying room temperatures. It's also a good idea to bring a light snack and a water bottle to help maintain your energy and focus throughout the exam.

- **Arriving at the testing center:** Plan to arrive at the testing center at least 30 minutes before your scheduled exam time. This will give you ample time to check in, find your seat, and settle before the exam begins.

- **Time management:** As previously mentioned, you'll have 4 hours to complete the 100-question exam. Be mindful of your time and pace yourself accordingly, spending approximately 1-2 minutes on each question. If you find yourself stuck on a difficult question, make an educated guess and move on, as you can always return to it later if time permits.

Post-Exam Information

- **Exam results:** The AAPC typically releases results within 7-10 business days following the exam date. You'll receive an email notification when your results are available, and you can view your score on the AAPC website.

- **Passing score:** To pass the CPC exam, you must achieve a minimum score of 70%. If you do not pass on your first attempt, you can take advantage of the free retake in your exam fee.

- **Continuing Education Units (CEUs):** Once you've earned your CPC certification, you'll need to maintain your credential by completing Continuing Education Units (CEUs) and renewing your AAPC membership annually. This ensures that you stay current with industry developments and continue growing professionally.

In conclusion, proper preparation and a thorough understanding of the CPC exam's structure and content are crucial for success. By developing a strategic study plan, using diverse resources, and employing effective test-taking strategies, you'll be well-equipped to tackle the exam and become a Certified Professional Coder.

CPC CODING TECHNIQUES

In this chapter, we will explore various CPC coding techniques that are essential for accurate and efficient medical coding. These techniques help you improve your coding skills and increase your chances of passing the CPC exam. By mastering these techniques, you'll become more confident and proficient in your coding abilities.

Understanding Coding Guidelines and Conventions

Before diving into coding techniques, it's crucial to have a solid understanding of coding guidelines and conventions. The ICD-10-CM, CPT, and HCPCS Level II coding systems have rules and guidelines that dictate how codes should be assigned and reported. Familiarizing yourself with these guidelines is essential for accurate coding and compliance.

- **ICD-10-CM:** The ICD-10-CM Official Guidelines for Coding and Reporting provide detailed instructions for assigning diagnosis codes based on medical record documentation. These guidelines cover general coding principles, such as code sequencing, principal diagnosis selection, and additional regulations to capture all relevant clinical information.
- **CPT:** The CPT coding system is governed by the American Medical Association (AMA) and is accompanied by guidelines that dictate how procedure codes should be reported. These guidelines include information on code selection, modifiers, and writing multiple procedures.
- **HCPCS Level II:** Developed by the Centers for Medicare & Medicaid Services (CMS), the HCPCS Level II coding system includes guidelines for reporting additional services, supplies, and equipment not covered by CPT codes. These guidelines help ensure accurate reporting of these items for reimbursement purposes.

Medical Terminology and Anatomy

A strong foundation in medical terminology and anatomy is essential for effective coding. Familiarize yourself with common medical prefixes, suffixes, and root words, as well as the structure and function of various body systems and organs. This knowledge will help you accurately interpret medical documentation and assign the appropriate codes.

Coding from Medical Records

One of the most essential CPC coding techniques is the ability to code directly from medical records. This skill involves reading and interpreting clinical documentation, such as physician notes, operative reports, and diagnostic studies, to determine the appropriate codes for diagnoses, procedures, and other services. When coding from medical records, follow these steps:

1. Read the entire document thoroughly to understand the patient's condition and the services provided.
2. Identify the principal diagnosis and the main reason for the patient's encounter with the healthcare provider. This should be coded first in the sequence of diagnosis codes.
3. Identify any additional diagnoses relevant to the patient's care and treatment. These should be coded in order of significance.
4. Determine the appropriate procedure codes based on the services provided, considering CPT guidelines for code selection and modifiers.
5. Assign any necessary HCPCS Level II codes for additional services, supplies, or equipment not covered by CPT codes.
6. Review your code selections to ensure they accurately represent the information provided in the medical record and adhere to coding guidelines and conventions.

Using Modifiers Correctly

Modifiers are an essential component of the CPT coding system and are used to provide additional information about a procedure or service. Proper use of modifiers is crucial for accurate coding and reimbursement. Some common modifiers include:

Modifier 59: Indicates a distinct procedural service. Use this modifier when reporting different, non-overlapping services performed during the same encounter.

Modifier 25: Indicates a significant, separately identifiable evaluation and management (E/M) service provided on the same day as another procedure or service.

Modifier 51: Indicates multiple procedures performed during the same session by the same provider.

To use modifiers effectively, review the CPT guidelines and the specific instructions for each modifier to ensure accurate reporting. When applying modifiers, always verify that the modifier is appropriate in the particular code and situation and provides the necessary information to describe the service or procedure accurately.

Staying Current with Coding Updates

The medical coding field constantly evolves, with annual updates to coding systems and guidelines. Staying current with these changes is crucial for accurate and compliant coding. To keep up-to-date with the latest updates:

1. Subscribe to coding newsletters and industry publications, such as the AAPC's Healthcare Business Monthly or the AMA's CPT Assistant, to receive information on coding changes and best practices.
2. Attend coding conferences, seminars, and webinars to learn from industry experts and stay informed on the latest developments in the field.
3. Participate in online forums and discussion groups to exchange knowledge and insights with fellow coding professionals.
4. Complete continuing education courses and earn Continuing Education Units (CEUs) to maintain your CPC certification and enhance your skills.

Time Management and Efficiency

Time management is essential for effective coding, particularly during the CPC exam. To improve your coding speed and accuracy:

1. Develop a systematic approach to coding, such as reviewing the medical record, identifying the principal diagnosis and additional diagnoses, determining the appropriate procedure codes, and assigning modifiers as needed.
2. Familiarize yourself with your coding manuals and know where to find important information, such as coding guidelines, instructions, and conventions. This will help you quickly locate the information required during the exam.
3. Practice coding real medical cases to build your speed and proficiency.
4. During the exam, focus on answering questions you're confident about first and then return to more challenging questions if time permits. This will help you maximize your chances of success by completing as many questions as possible within the allotted time.

Quality Assurance and Compliance

Ensuring accurate and compliant coding is crucial for healthcare providers to receive appropriate reimbursement and avoid potential audits or penalties. To maintain quality assurance and compliance in your coding:

1. Review coding guidelines and conventions to ensure your coding practices are up-to-date and by industry standards.
2. Perform regular audits of your coding work to identify any errors or inconsistencies and address them promptly.
3. Seek feedback from colleagues and supervisors to identify areas for improvement and enhance your coding skills.

In conclusion, mastering CPC coding techniques is essential for success in the medical coding field and on the CPC exam. By understanding coding guidelines and conventions, building a solid medical terminology and anatomy foundation, and developing effective coding and time management skills, you'll be well-equipped to excel in your profession and become a Certified Professional Coder.

Use of Billing Codes

In this section, we will discuss the use of billing codes, which play a crucial role in medical billing and reimbursement. Billing codes report diagnoses, procedures, and other healthcare services provided to patients, allowing healthcare providers to receive appropriate payment. Understanding billing codes correctly is essential for accurate and compliant medical coding.

Diagnosis Codes

Diagnosis codes, represented by the ICD-10-CM coding system, report a patient's medical conditions and diagnoses. These codes provide detailed information about the patient's health and the reasons for their encounter with the healthcare provider. When assigning diagnosis codes:

1. Identify the principal diagnosis and the main reason for the patient's encounter. This should be coded first in the sequence of diagnosis codes.
2. Assign additional diagnosis codes for coexisting conditions that may impact the patient's care or treatment. These should be coded in order of significance.
3. Review the ICD-10-CM Official Guidelines for Coding and Reporting to ensure proper code selection and sequencing.
4. Be specific and accurate when assigning diagnosis codes, using the highest level of detail available in the coding system.

Procedure Codes

Procedure codes, represented by the CPT coding system, report medical procedures, services, and interventions performed by healthcare providers. These codes describe the specific services provided to the patient and are essential for accurate reimbursement. When assigning procedure codes:

1. Determine the appropriate CPT code(s) based on the medical documentation and the services provided.
2. Review the CPT guidelines for information on code selection, the use of modifiers, and reporting multiple procedures.
3. Ensure the selected procedure codes accurately represent the services performed and adhere to the CPT guidelines and conventions.
4. Apply appropriate modifiers, if needed, to provide additional information about the procedure or service.

HCPCS Level II Codes

HCPCS Level II codes report additional services, supplies, and equipment not covered by CPT codes. These codes are essential for billing Medicare, Medicaid, and some private insurance carriers for services and items not included in the CPT coding system. When assigning HCPCS Level II codes:

1. Determine if a specific HCPCS Level II code is required for the service, supply, or equipment documented in the medical record.
2. Review the HCPCS Level II guidelines for information on code selection and the use of modifiers.
3. Ensure the selected HCPCS Level II codes accurately represent the services or items provided and adhere to the relevant guidelines and conventions.
4. If needed, apply appropriate HCPCS Level II modifiers to provide additional information about the service or item.

Ensuring Accurate and Compliant Billing

Proper use of billing codes is essential for accurate and compliant medical billing. To ensure that your coding practices meet industry standards:

1. Review coding guidelines and conventions for ICD-10-CM, CPT, and HCPCS Level II codes.
2. Perform regular audits of your coding work to identify and address any errors or inconsistencies.
3. Seek feedback from colleagues and supervisors to improve your coding skills and knowledge continuously.
4. Stay current with industry updates, including changes to coding systems, guidelines, and payer-specific requirements.

By understanding and effectively using billing codes, you'll be well-equipped to accurately report diagnoses, procedures, and other healthcare services, ensuring proper reimbursement for healthcare providers and compliance with industry standards.

Effective CPC Coding Techniques and Strategies

In this section, we will explore effective CPC coding techniques and strategies to help you improve your coding skills and boost your chances of success on the CPC exam. By mastering these techniques, you'll become more efficient and confident in your coding abilities, setting the foundation for a successful career as a Certified Professional Coder.

Know Your Coding Manuals

Familiarity with your coding manuals is essential for efficient and accurate coding. Spend time reviewing the ICD-10-CM, CPT, and HCPCS Level II manuals, paying particular attention to the guidelines, conventions, and instructions that govern each coding system. Knowing where to find crucial information quickly will help you save time during the exam and daily work.

Practice with Real-Life Scenarios

Practicing with real-life medical cases is one of the most effective ways to improve your coding skills. Work through various case scenarios that cover a wide range of medical conditions, procedures, and specialties. This will help you gain experience in interpreting medical documentation, selecting appropriate codes, and applying coding guidelines and conventions.

Develop a Systematic Approach

Developing a systematic approach to coding can help you become more efficient and accurate. For example, when coding from a medical record:

1. Read the entire document thoroughly to understand the patient's condition and the services provided.
2. Identify the principal diagnosis and any additional diagnoses in order of significance.
3. Determine the appropriate procedure codes based on the services provided.
4. Assign any necessary HCPCS Level II codes for additional services, supplies, or equipment.
5. Review your code selections to ensure they accurately represent the information provided in the medical record and adhere to coding guidelines and conventions.

Utilize Time Management Techniques

Effective time management is critical for success on the CPC exam and daily work. To improve your coding speed and accuracy:

1. Set a timer while practicing coding scenarios to simulate the time constraints of the exam.
2. Focus on answering questions you're confident about first, then return to more challenging questions if time permits.
3. Develop a plan for navigating the exam, such as starting with the section you're most comfortable with or tackling questions with the highest point value first.

Continuously Expand Your Knowledge

Staying up-to-date with industry developments, coding updates, and best practices is crucial for success in the medical coding field. To expand your knowledge:

1. Participate in continuing education courses and earn Continuing Education Units (CEUs) to maintain your CPC certification.
2. Attend coding conferences, seminars, and webinars to learn from industry experts.
3. Engage in online forums and discussion groups to exchange knowledge and insights with fellow coding professionals.

Seek Feedback and Support

Seeking feedback from colleagues and supervisors can help you identify areas for improvement and enhance your coding skills. Feel free to ask for help or clarification when needed, as this can provide valuable insights and prevent potential errors in your coding work.

In summary, by implementing effective CPC coding techniques and strategies, you'll be well-equipped to excel in your profession and succeed on the CPC exam. Mastery of these techniques will not only improve your coding skills and boost your confidence, setting the stage for a successful career as a Certified Professional Coder.

Examples of CPC Coding Cases

In this section, we will provide examples of CPC coding cases to illustrate the application of coding principles and techniques in real-life scenarios. These examples will help you better understand how to approach different medical issues and apply the appropriate codes based on the information provided in the medical documentation.

Example 1: Acute Bronchitis with Asthma

Patient: 45-year-old female
Chief Complaint: Shortness of breath and cough
Diagnoses: Acute bronchitis, moderate persistent asthma
Treatment: Albuterol nebulizer treatment, prescription for oral steroids

Review the ICD-10-CM codes for the principal diagnosis (acute bronchitis) and additional diagnosis (moderate persistent asthma).

Acute bronchitis: J20.9
Moderate persistent asthma: J45.41
Determine the appropriate CPT code for the nebulizer treatment.

Albuterol nebulizer treatment: 94664
Assign the necessary HCPCS Level II code for the prescribed oral steroids.

Oral steroids: No specific HCPCS Level II code is required, as these medications are typically self-administered and billed through a pharmacy.

Final Codes:

J20.9 (Acute bronchitis)
J45.41 (Moderate persistent asthma)
94664 (Albuterol nebulizer treatment)

Example 2: Laparoscopic Cholecystectomy

Patient: 52-year-old male
Chief Complaint: Abdominal pain
Diagnoses: Cholelithiasis, acute cholecystitis
Procedure: Laparoscopic cholecystectomy

Review the ICD-10-CM codes for the principal diagnosis (cholelithiasis) and additional diagnosis (acute cholecystitis).

Cholelithiasis: K80.20
Acute cholecystitis: K81.0
Determine the appropriate CPT code for the laparoscopic cholecystectomy.

Laparoscopic cholecystectomy: 47562

Final Codes:

K80.20 (Cholelithiasis)
K81.0 (Acute cholecystitis)
47562 (Laparoscopic cholecystectomy)

Example 3: Evaluation and Management of Hypertension

Patient: 60-year-old female
Chief Complaint: High blood pressure
Diagnoses: Essential hypertension
Procedure: Evaluation and management, prescription for antihypertensive medication

Review the ICD-10-CM code for the principal diagnosis (essential hypertension).

Essential hypertension: I10
Determine the appropriate CPT code for the evaluation and management visit.

Established patient, office visit, moderate complexity: 99214
Assign the necessary HCPCS Level II code for the prescribed antihypertensive medication.

Antihypertensive medication: No specific HCPCS Level II code is required, as these medications are typically self-administered and billed through a pharmacy.

Final Codes:

I10 (Essential hypertension)
99214 (Evaluation and management, moderate complexity)

These examples demonstrate applying coding principles and techniques to various medical scenarios. Practice with more case examples to improve your coding skills and build confidence in your ability to assign correct codes based on the information provided in medical documentation. Always follow each coding system's coding guidelines, conventions, and instructions, and consult your coding manuals as needed.

LAWS AND REGULATIONS

As a Certified Professional Coder, it's essential to have a thorough understanding of the laws and regulations governing medical coding and billing. In this chapter, we will discuss the most relevant laws and regulations that impact the medical coding profession, as well as the role of the Certified Professional Coder in ensuring compliance with these legal requirements.

Health Insurance Portability and Accountability Act (HIPAA)

HIPAA is a federal law enacted in 1996 that establishes national standards for the privacy and security of patients' protected health information (PHI). HIPAA impacts the medical coding profession by requiring strict adherence to privacy and security regulations when handling PHI, including:

1. Ensuring that PHI is only accessed and disclosed to authorized individuals for approved purposes.
2. Implementing safeguards to protect PHI from unauthorized access, use, or disclosure.
3. Providing patients access to medical records and the right to request amendments or corrections.
4. Reporting breaches of PHI to the appropriate authorities.

As a Certified Professional Coder, you must be familiar with HIPAA's privacy and security regulations and ensure that your coding practices adhere to these requirements to protect patient privacy.

False Claims Act (FCA)

The False Claims Act is a federal law that prohibits submitting false or fraudulent claims for payment to government healthcare programs such as Medicare and Medicaid. Under the FCA, medical coders and other healthcare professionals can be held legally responsible for submitting false claims if they knowingly or recklessly:

1. Assign incorrect codes to inflate reimbursement.
2. Unbundle codes to increase payment.
3. Bill for services not provided or not medically necessary.

To avoid potential violations of the FCA, Certified Professional Coders must ensure that their coding practices are accurate, ethical, and compliant with all applicable coding guidelines and regulations.

Medicare and Medicaid Regulations

Medicare and Medicaid are government healthcare programs that provide coverage for millions of Americans. These programs are subject to complex laws and regulations governing coverage, reimbursement, and coding practices. Some key aspects of Medicare and Medicaid regulations that impact medical coding include:

1. **Coverage policies:** Coders must be familiar with the coverage policies for the services they code to ensure that claims are submitted correctly and in compliance with program requirements.
2. **Correct coding initiatives:** Medicare and Medicaid employ various coding initiatives to prevent fraud, waste, and abuse. These initiatives include the National Correct Coding Initiative (NCCI), which sets coding edits and guidelines to ensure accurate billing.
3. **Documentation requirements:** Medicare and Medicaid have specific documentation requirements for services rendered. Coders must ensure that the medical records they review meet these requirements to support the codes assigned and justify reimbursement.

Certified Professional Coders must stay up-to-date with Medicare and Medicaid regulations changes and incorporate these requirements into their coding practices to ensure compliance.

Office of Inspector General (OIG) Compliance Program Guidance

The Office of Inspector General (OIG) is an agency within the U.S. Department of Health and Human Services responsible for detecting and preventing fraud, waste, and abuse within federal healthcare programs. The OIG has published Compliance Program Guidance for various healthcare industry segments, including hospitals, nursing facilities, and physician practices.

The OIG's Compliance Program Guidance provides a framework for healthcare organizations to develop and implement an effective compliance program that addresses potential risk areas, including medical coding and billing. Critical components of a compliance program include:

1. Implementing written policies and procedures.
2. Designating a compliance officer and compliance committee.
3. Providing ongoing education and training.
4. Conducting regular audits and monitoring.
5. Establishing a system for reporting potential compliance issues.
6. Responding promptly to detected issues and taking corrective action.
7. Enforcing disciplinary standards and consequences for non-compliance.

As a Certified Professional Coder, you may be involved in your organization's compliance program by participating in ongoing education, conducting internal audits, and adhering to your organization's policies and procedures related to medical coding and billing.

State Laws and Regulations

In addition to federal laws and regulations, medical coders must be familiar with state-specific statutes and regulations governing medical coding and billing. These may include:

1. **State-specific Medicaid regulations:** Each state administers its own Medicaid program and may have unique rules and guidelines that impact medical coding practices.
2. **Provider licensure and scope of practice regulations:** State laws define the scope of practice for various healthcare providers, which may impact coding and billing for services provided by these professionals.
3. **State-specific privacy laws:** Some states have enacted privacy laws that provide additional protections for patients' medical information beyond what is required under HIPAA.

To ensure compliance with state laws and regulations, Certified Professional Coders should consult their state's Department of Health or other relevant agencies for guidance and resources.

Professional Ethics and the AAPC Code of Ethics

As a Certified Professional Coder, you are also bound by the professional ethics and standards set forth by the AAPC, which certifies medical coders. The AAPC Code of Ethics outlines the principles and values that should guide the conduct of medical coders, including:

1. **Integrity:** Coders should demonstrate honesty, accuracy, and objectivity.
2. **Respect for privacy:** Coders should maintain patient medical information confidentiality by HIPAA and other applicable laws and regulations.
3. **Professional development:** Coders should pursue ongoing education and training to maintain and enhance their coding skills and knowledge.
4. **Compliance:** Coders should adhere to all relevant laws, regulations, guidelines, and professional standards that govern medical coding and billing.
5. **By adhering to the AAPC Code of Ethics**, Certified Professional Coders can help ensure that their coding practices meet the highest standards of professionalism, accuracy, and compliance.

In conclusion, understanding and adhering to the relevant laws and regulations governing medical coding and billing is critical to the Certified Professional Coder's role. This chapter has provided an overview of the legal and regulatory frameworks impacting the medical coding profession. By staying informed of these requirements and incorporating them into your coding practices, you can help ensure your work's accuracy, compliance, and integrity as a Certified Professional Coder.

Industry Legislation

Several critical pieces of legislation have been enacted in the medical coding and billing industry to ensure patients' and healthcare providers' safety, privacy, and financial security. This section will explore some of the most influential and relevant industry legislation that directly impacts Certified Professional Coders and their day-to-day responsibilities.

Affordable Care Act (ACA)

The Affordable Care Act, commonly known as Obamacare, was signed into law in 2010 to improve access to affordable healthcare for all Americans. Some aspects of the ACA that impact medical coding professionals include:

Expansion of insurance coverage: The ACA has expanded access to health insurance by creating state and federal health insurance marketplaces and developing Medicaid programs in many states. This has increased the number of insured patients and resulted in a higher demand for accurate medical coding and billing services.

Value-based reimbursement models: The ACA has introduced several value-based reimbursement programs, such as the Hospital Readmissions Reduction Program and the Hospital Value-Based Purchasing Program. These programs incentivize healthcare providers to deliver high-quality care by tying reimbursement to performance on specific quality measures. Medical coders are crucial in accurately documenting and reporting these quality measures.

Health Information Technology for Economic and Clinical Health Act (HITECH)

The HITECH Act was enacted in 2009 to promote the adoption and meaningful use of health information technology, particularly electronic health records (EHRs). The HITECH Act has several implications for medical coders, including:

- **Increased use of EHRs:** As more healthcare providers adopt EHR systems, medical coders must become proficient in accessing and reviewing patient records for coding purposes.

- **Enhanced privacy and security:** The HITECH Act strengthens the privacy and security provisions of HIPAA by introducing new requirements for breach notification and increased penalties for non-compliance. Medical coders must know these requirements and ensure their coding practices align with these enhanced protections.

21st Century Cures Act

The 21st Century Cures Act, signed into law in 2016, aims to accelerate the development and approval of innovative medical treatments, improve mental health services, and increase access to healthcare. Some provisions of the Cures Act that impact medical coding professionals include:

Interoperability and information sharing: The Cures Act promotes the seamless exchange of health information between healthcare providers, which can improve the accuracy and efficiency of medical coding processes.

Advancing precision medicine: The Cures Act supports the development of personalized, data-driven healthcare treatments, which may require new coding and billing practices to accommodate these innovative therapies.

Federal and state regulations

As a Certified Professional Coder, staying informed about industry legislation and its impact on medical coding and billing practices is essential. By understanding these laws and adapting your coding practices accordingly, you can help ensure compliance and improve healthcare delivery and patient outcomes.

Federal and State Regulations

As a Certified Professional Coder, staying informed about federal and state regulations that govern the medical coding and billing industry is crucial. These regulations significantly ensure patient privacy, accurate billing practices, and compliance with various laws. This section will explore some critical federal and state regulations directly impacting medical coding professionals.

Federal Regulations

Several federal agencies and organizations are responsible for creating and enforcing regulations that impact medical coding practices. Some of the most relevant federal laws include:

- **Centers for Medicare & Medicaid Services (CMS):** CMS is the federal agency that oversees the Medicare and Medicaid programs. They establish rules, guidelines, and reimbursement rates for patient services under these programs. As a medical coder, it's essential to understand CMS regulations and ensure that your coding practices adhere to their requirements.

- **Office of the Inspector General (OIG):** The OIG is responsible for identifying and combatting fraud, waste, and abuse within the healthcare system, including medical coding and billing practices. They issue guidance on compliance programs and recommend best practices for healthcare organizations to reduce the risk of fraudulent or non-compliant billing.

- **National Correct Coding Initiative (NCCI):** The NCCI is a CMS program to promote accurate coding and prevent improper payments for Medicare Part B services. NCCI edits are automated prepayment claim edits that identify coding inconsistencies and potential errors. Medical coders should be familiar with NCCI guidelines and follow these edits to ensure accurate and compliant coding.

State Regulations

In addition to federal regulations, medical coders must be aware of state-specific rules governing medical coding and billing practices. These regulations can vary from state to state and may include:

State Medicaid regulations: Each state administers its own Medicaid program, which may have unique rules and guidelines for medical coding and billing. Medical coders should familiarize themselves with the Medicaid regulations in their state to ensure compliance.

Provider licensure and scope of practice regulations: State laws govern the licensure and scope of practice for healthcare providers, which may impact coding and billing for services provided by these professionals. Medical coders should understand the scope of practice rules for providers in their state and code services accordingly.

State-specific privacy laws: Some states have enacted privacy laws that provide additional protections for patients' medical information beyond what is required under HIPAA. Medical coders should know state-specific privacy laws and ensure their coding practices meet these requirements.

In conclusion, understanding and adhering to federal and state regulations is critical to the Certified Professional Coder's role. By staying informed of these regulations and incorporating them into your coding practices, you can help ensure your work's accuracy, compliance, and integrity. Furthermore, being proactive in seeking relevant updates and resources can contribute to your professional development and help you stay current in the ever-evolving field of medical coding.

Compliance Processes

Compliance is a critical component of the medical coding profession, as it ensures adherence to laws, regulations, and industry standards that protect patients and healthcare providers. In this section, we will discuss the importance of compliance processes and provide practical guidance on how Certified Professional Coders can contribute to a culture of compliance within their organizations.

The Importance of Compliance

A robust compliance program is essential for healthcare organizations to mitigate risks, prevent fraud, maintain the trust of patients and payers, and avoid potential legal and financial consequences. For medical coders, understanding the importance of compliance and being proactive in ensuring that coding practices align with established guidelines is crucial to professional success.

The benefits of a robust compliance program include:

- **Accurate and timely reimbursement:** When coding practices comply with regulations and guidelines, the likelihood of receiving accurate and timely refunds from payers increases, ensuring the organization's financial health.

- **Reduced risk of audits and penalties:** Adhering to compliance processes can help prevent audits and potential financial penalties associated with non-compliant coding practices.

- **Enhanced patient trust and satisfaction:** Compliance with privacy regulations, such as HIPAA, helps protect sensitive patient information and maintains patients' confidence in the healthcare organization.

- **Improved quality of care:** Accurate coding and documentation enable healthcare providers to make well-informed decisions about patient care and treatment plans.

Developing a Compliance Program

Creating a comprehensive compliance program is a multi-step process that requires input and participation from various stakeholders within a healthcare organization. Critical elements of an effective compliance program include:

- **Written policies and procedures:** Establish clear policies and procedures outlining the organization's commitment to compliance and providing specific guidance for coding and billing processes.

- **Compliance officer and committee:** Appoint a designated compliance officer and establish a compliance committee to oversee the implementation and ongoing maintenance of the compliance program.

- **Training and education:** Provide regular training and education for all staff members, including medical coders, on relevant regulations, guidelines, and best practices to ensure a clear understanding of their roles and responsibilities in maintaining compliance.

- **Internal monitoring and auditing:** Implement routine internal monitoring and auditing processes to identify potential coding errors or non-compliant practices and address them proactively.

- **Disciplinary guidelines:** Develop precise disciplinary approaches to address non-compliant behavior or actions that violate the organization's policies and procedures.

- **Open communication channels:** Encourage open communication among staff members to discuss potential compliance concerns and provide a mechanism for anonymous reporting of suspected violations.

- **Prompt response and corrective action:** Establish a process for promptly addressing identified compliance issues and implementing disciplinary actions to prevent recurrence.

The Role of the Certified Professional Coder in Compliance

As a Certified Professional Coder, you support your organization's compliance efforts. Here are some practical steps you can take to contribute to a culture of compliance:

- **Stay informed:** Regularly review industry updates, attend training sessions, and participate in professional development opportunities to stay current on relevant laws, regulations, and guidelines.

- **Follow established policies and procedures:** Adhere to your organization's established coding policies and procedures and consult with the compliance officer or committee if you encounter any uncertainties or challenges.

- **Advocate for compliance:** Encourage your colleagues to prioritize compliance and support them in adhering to established guidelines and best practices.

- **Participate in internal audits and monitoring:** Be proactive in identifying potential coding errors or non-compliant practices, and collaborate with the compliance team to address any issues promptly.

- **Report concerns:** If you suspect a potential violation of your organization's compliance policies, report your problems to the appropriate parties, such as the compliance officer or committee, or use established anonymous reporting channels

- **Foster a culture of continuous improvement:** Encourage open dialogue with your colleagues about best practices and areas for improvement in coding and compliance processes. Share your insights and expertise to help enhance the organization's compliance efforts.

- **Collaborate with other departments:** Build strong working relationships with other departments, such as billing, clinical staff, and administration, to ensure everyone works together to maintain compliance.

- **Be proactive in addressing potential issues:** If you identify a trend or pattern of coding errors or non-compliant practices, proactively address the problem by providing additional training, clarifying policies, or implementing new procedures to prevent future occurrences.

- **Document your work:** Maintain thorough documentation of your coding decisions and actions, which can serve as valuable evidence of your organization's commitment to compliance during an audit or investigation.

- **Support the development and refinement of your organization's compliance program:** As a Certified Professional Coder, your insights and expertise can be invaluable in shaping and refining your organization's compliance program. Offer your feedback and suggestions to help improve the program's effectiveness and ensure that it is responsive to your workplace's unique needs and challenges.

In summary, a solid commitment to compliance is essential for Certified Professional Coders and their healthcare organizations. By staying informed, following established policies and procedures, and actively participating in your organization's compliance efforts, you can help ensure your coding practices' accuracy, integrity, and success. Additionally, your ongoing engagement in compliance processes will contribute to the overall financial health and reputation of your organization while also promoting patient trust and satisfaction.

TOOLS AND TECHNOLOGY

In today's fast-paced and technologically advanced healthcare environment, Certified Professional Coders must stay up-to-date with the latest tools and technologies that can enhance the accuracy and efficiency of their work. This chapter will explore various tools and technologies that can support CPCs in their daily tasks, including Electronic Health Record (EHR) systems, coding software, billing software, and other resources to help streamline the coding and billing process.

Electronic Health Record Systems

Electronic Health Record (EHR) systems have revolutionized how healthcare providers manage and access patient information. These digital platforms offer a range of features that can significantly improve the efficiency and accuracy of medical coding, including:

Centralized access to patient data: EHR systems consolidate all patient information, including medical history, diagnostic test results, and treatment plans, making it easier for CPCs to locate the information required for accurate coding.

Automated code suggestions: Some EHR systems include built-in coding tools that suggest appropriate codes based on the information entered by healthcare providers. While a certified coder should always verify these suggestions, they can save time and reduce the risk of errors.

Enhanced documentation: EHR systems often include templates and structured data entry fields that guide healthcare providers in creating thorough, accurate, and consistent documentation, making the coding process more efficient.

Interoperability: EHR systems can communicate with other healthcare systems and software, facilitating seamless data exchange and reducing the need for manual data entry.

Coding Software

Coding software is an essential tool for CPCs, as it offers a wide range of features that can streamline the coding process and improve accuracy. Some popular coding software options include:

Encoder software: Encoder software offers access to the most current versions of the ICD, CPT, and HCPCS code sets, along with valuable resources such as coding guidelines, instructional notes, and decision-support tools. Encoders can also automate the code selection process based on the entered documentation, though it's crucial for CPCs to verify these suggestions.

Code reference software: Code reference software provides an easy-to-use interface for quickly looking up specific codes and guidelines, making it a valuable resource for CPCs who need to verify codes or find additional information during the coding process.

Specialty-specific coding software: Some software solutions are tailored to specific medical specialties, offering in-depth resources and tools that address these specialties' unique coding challenges and requirements.

Billing Software

Medical billing software is another essential tool for CPCs, as it helps manage the claims submission and reimbursement process. Critical features of medical billing software include:

Claim creation and submission: Billing software simplifies creating and submitting claims by automatically generating claim forms based on the entered codes and patient information.

Electronic remittance advice (ERA): ERAs are electronic versions of Explanation of Benefits (EOB) statements that detail the amounts paid by payers on submitted claims. Billing software can receive and process ERAs, streamlining the process of posting payments and reconciling accounts.

Claim tracking and follow-up: Billing software offers tools for tracking the status of submitted claims and identifying issues that may require follow-up, such as denied or rejected claims.

Reporting and analytics: Many billing software solutions include reporting and analytics tools that allow CPCs to track key performance indicators, such as claim submission and denial rates, to identify areas for improvement and optimize revenue cycle performance.

Additional Tools and Resources

In addition to EHR systems, coding software, and billing software, there are a variety of other tools and resources that can support CPCs in their work:

Online forums and communities: Online forums, such as the AAPC community, offer a platform for CPCs to connect with their peers, share experiences, and seek advice on coding challenges and best practices. Participating in these forums can help CPCs stay informed about industry trends and expand their professional networks.

Webinars and training courses: Ongoing education is essential for CPCs to stay up-to-date with the latest coding guidelines, regulations, and best practices. Many organizations, including the AAPC, offer webinars, training courses, and continuing education opportunities covering various coding-related topics.

Mobile apps: Several mobile apps can provide quick access to code sets, guidelines, and other resources for CPCs on the go. These apps can be a convenient resource for busy professionals who need to access coding information quickly and easily.

Coding newsletters and blogs: Keeping informed about industry news and trends is crucial for CPCs to remain current and competitive. Subscribing to coding newsletters and following relevant blogs can help ensure you're always aware of the latest medical coding and healthcare regulations and developments.

Embracing Technology in the Coding Profession

As a Certified Professional Coder, integrating these various tools and technologies into your daily workflow can have several advantages, such as improved productivity, accuracy, and compliance. But it's crucial to remember that technology should never replace a qualified coder's critical thinking and knowledge.

As a CPC, you are responsible for using these tools to improve your job and make better-educated coding decisions, constantly keeping an eye out for the little things and a dedication to correctness. You can ensure you're well-equipped to succeed in the dynamic and quickly expanding world of medical coding by remaining knowledgeable on the most recent tools and technologies and using those that best complement your job.

Data Management Software

A Certified Professional Coder's everyday activities depend heavily on data management software and EHR systems, coding software, and billing software. Effective data management is essential to guarantee that the coding process is precise, efficient, and in compliance with industry standards and laws. The benefits of various types of data management software for CPCs will be covered in this section.

Tools for reporting and data analytics: As a CPC, you'll maintain and analyze vast amounts of patient data and coding data. You may explore the overall coding performance of your business, spot areas for improvement, and find trends and patterns using data analytics and reporting tools. These solutions frequently provide configurable dashboards and reports, enabling you to concentrate on the most pertinent and helpful information for your particular requirements.

Systematic storage, organization, and access to all forms of electronic documents, such as patient records, coding standards, and policies and procedures, are provided by document management systems. These systems frequently include powerful search capabilities that make it simple for CPCs to find the data they want for precise and effective coding. By providing features like version control, access restrictions, and audit trails, document management systems may also assist in ensuring compliance with industry requirements.

Data integration tools: By combining data from numerous sources, including EHR systems, billing software, and external databases, data integration solutions can assist in speeding the coding process. These technologies can assist CPCs in making better-informed coding decisions and lower the possibility of mistakes brought on by missing or incorrect information by giving a unified picture of all pertinent data.

Tools for data validation: Accurate and compliant coding depends on the quality and completeness of patient data. Data input mistakes, inconsistencies, and omissions may be found and fixed using data validation tools, enhancing the accuracy of the data used for coding and billing. Data entry forms with built-in validation criteria, automatic data quality checks, and reporting tools to track the evolution of data quality are a few examples of features that these tools could include.

Data security tools: It is crucial for healthcare organizations and their workers, especially CPCs, to protect the confidentiality, integrity, and availability of patient data. Data security technologies can help reduce the risk of data breaches, unauthorized access, and other security events by ensuring your organization's data is stored, communicated, and accessed securely. Some examples of these technologies are software for encryption, access control, and network security.

Solutions for data backup and recovery: Having a dependable backup and recovery solution in place is crucial for ensuring business continuity and protecting your organization's data in the case of a system failure, data loss, or other unforeseen catastrophes. Depending on your firm's particular requirements and risk tolerance, these solutions can comprise local backup systems, cloud-based backup services, or a combination of the two.

In conclusion, efficient data management is a crucial step in the coding process. Investing in the appropriate tools and technology may boost your coding operations' productivity, accuracy, and compliance. You can guarantee that you are well-prepared to succeed as a Certified Data Management Professional by being familiar with the many types of data management software available and choosing the solutions that best match your organization's needs.

Automation Tools

Automation has become an increasingly important aspect of the healthcare industry, and its impact on medical coding is no exception. By leveraging automation tools, Certified Professional Coders (CPCs) can streamline workflows, improve accuracy, and increase productivity. This section will discuss various automation tools that can benefit CPCs' day-to-day tasks.

Computer-Assisted Coding (CAC) systems: CAC systems utilize Natural Language Processing (NLP) technology to analyze and interpret medical documentation, automatically generating suggested codes based on the content of the records. These suggestions can then be reviewed and validated by a CPC, which can save time and help reduce the risk of errors. CAC systems can also help identify gaps in documentation, prompting physicians to provide additional information when necessary.

Robotic Process Automation (RPA): RPA software uses artificial intelligence and machine learning algorithms to perform repetitive, rule-based tasks typically completed by human coders. By automating these tasks, RPA can help CPC focus on more complex coding scenarios and higher-value tasks. Examples of functions that can be automated using RPA include data entry, claim processing, and routine data validation.

Code prediction tools: Some software solutions incorporate machine learning algorithms to predict the most likely codes for a given case based on historical coding patterns and trends. By providing these predictions to CPCs, code prediction tools can help guide their decision-making process and improve overall coding accuracy.

Automated code auditing: Auditing is an essential aspect of the coding process, ensuring that codes are accurate, compliant, and submitted promptly. Automated code auditing tools can help streamline this process by automatically reviewing coded records for potential errors, inconsistencies, and compliance issues. These tools can also generate reports and analytics to help CPC identify trends, track performance, and implement targeted improvement initiatives.

Workflow automation software can help CPCs manage their coding tasks more efficiently by automating routine processes and organizing tasks according to priority. These solutions often include features such as task assignment, deadline tracking, and notifications, enabling CPCs to stay on top of their workloads and ensure that tasks are completed promptly.

Automated code mapping: Many healthcare organizations use multiple code sets, such as ICD, CPT, and HCPCS, to describe various aspects of care. Automated code mapping tools can help simplify this process by automatically identifying equivalent codes across different sets, reducing the risk of errors and inconsistencies in coding and billing.

Artificial intelligence-powered tools: As AI technology advances, more tools and solutions are being developed specifically for the medical coding industry. These tools may include AI-powered code prediction, automated documentation analysis, and intelligent code auditing. By incorporating AI-powered tools into their workflows, CPCs can benefit from increased efficiency, accuracy, and compliance.

In conclusion, automation tools offer significant benefits for Certified Professional Coders, including increased efficiency, improved accuracy, and reduced risk of errors. By staying informed about the latest automation technologies and incorporating them into their daily workflows, CPCs can ensure that they remain competitive in the rapidly evolving field of medical coding. It is important to note that while automation tools can significantly enhance the coding process, they should be able to maintain a skilled human coder's expertise and critical thinking skills. Instead, these tools should be used to support and augment the work of CPCs, enabling them to focus on more complex and high-value tasks.

CAREER ADVICE

A Certified Professional Coder (CPC) 's career path can be rewarding and challenging. As a CPC, you'll have the opportunity to positively impact the healthcare industry by ensuring accurate coding and billing practices. However, like any other profession, navigating your career as a CPC requires dedication, hard work, and a strategic approach. This chapter will provide valuable career advice to help you excel as a CPC and maximize your professional opportunities.

Building a Strong Foundation

Education and certification are crucial components of a successful career in medical coding. Begin by pursuing a reputable educational program in medical coding, which will provide you with the necessary knowledge and skills to succeed in the field. Once you have completed your education, focus on obtaining your CPC certification from the AAPC. This credential demonstrates your commitment to the profession and validates your expertise in medical coding.

Networking and Professional Development

Networking plays a vital role in advancing your career as a CPC. Join professional associations like the AAPC and attend industry conferences and events to expand your professional network. Connecting with fellow professionals will give you access to new job opportunities, valuable insights, and mentorship. Additionally, consider participating in online forums and social media groups related to medical coding to stay informed about industry trends and developments.

Continuing professional development is also essential for a successful career as a CPC. Stay current with coding guidelines, regulations, and technology changes by pursuing ongoing education and training. Additional certifications, such as the Certified Inpatient Coder (CIC) or Certified Risk Adjustment Coder (CRC), can help you further specialize and enhance your marketability.

Gaining Experience and Building Your Portfolio

Hands-on experience is critical for developing your skills and improving your job prospects. Seek entry-level positions, internships, or volunteer opportunities to gain practical coding experience. As you gain experience, document your accomplishments and projects in a professional portfolio. This portfolio will serve as a tangible representation of your skills and expertise when applying for new positions or negotiating promotions.

Identifying and Pursuing Your Ideal Career Path

As a CPC, you can choose from various career paths, including inpatient and outpatient coding, risk adjustment coding, or auditing. Take the time to explore these options and determine which best aligns with your interests and long-term career goals. Once you've identified your preferred career path, tailor your education, certifications, and experience to position yourself for success.

Cultivating Soft Skills

While technical coding knowledge is vital, soft skills are equally crucial for a successful career as a CPC. Develop and refine your communication, critical thinking, and problem-solving skills. These skills will enable you to collaborate effectively with colleagues, quickly adapt to changes in the industry, and excel in your role.

Seeking Mentorship

A mentor can provide invaluable guidance and support throughout your career as a CPC. Seek a seasoned professional who can offer insights, advice, and encouragement. A mentor can help you navigate challenges, identify new opportunities, and develop your skills.

Setting and Achieving Career Goals

Establishing clear career goals is crucial for staying focused and motivated as a CPC. Consider your short-term and long-term objectives, such as obtaining additional certifications, specializing in a specific coding area, or advancing to a management role. Develop a plan to achieve these goals, and regularly evaluate your progress to stay on track.

Balancing Work-Life Integration

As a CPC, you may encounter demanding workloads and tight deadlines, leading to stress and burnout. It's essential to prioritize self-care and maintain a healthy work-life balance. Set boundaries, establish a routine, and make time for hobbies and personal interests outside of work. Additionally, focus on cultivating strong relationships with your colleagues, as a supportive work environment can significantly contribute to your overall well-being and job satisfaction.

Staying Adaptable and Embracing Change

The healthcare industry is continuously evolving, and as a CPC, it's crucial to stay adaptable and open to change. Stay informed about industry developments and trends, and be prepared to adjust your skills and knowledge accordingly. Embracing change and maintaining a growth mindset will enable you to stay competitive and thrive in your career.

Building Your Brand

Developing a solid personal brand can help you stand out in the competitive job market and attract new opportunities. Focus on highlighting your unique skills, expertise, and accomplishments through your resume, LinkedIn profile, and other professional channels. Regularly share relevant articles and insights on social media to showcase your industry knowledge and establish yourself as a thought leader in medical coding.

Navigating Challenges and Overcoming Obstacles

In your career as a CPC, you may face challenges such as complex coding cases, increased workload, or regulation changes. Approach these challenges positively and view them as opportunities for growth and learning. Seek support from colleagues, mentors, and professional networks, and be bold and ask for help when needed.

In conclusion, a successful career as a Certified Professional Coder requires education, certification, experience, and ongoing professional development. By following the advice outlined in this chapter, you can confidently navigate your career, overcome obstacles, and ultimately achieve your professional goals in the ever-evolving world of medical coding.

Required Skills and Competencies

To excel as a Certified Professional Coder (CPC), you must possess specific skills and competencies. These skills are essential for effectively navigating the complex world of medical coding and billing, and they can significantly contribute to your success in the field. In this section, we'll explore the crucial skills and competencies that every CPC should possess.

- **Coding Proficiency:** As a CPC, your primary responsibility is to code medical diagnoses, procedures, and services accurately. This requires a deep understanding of coding guidelines, conventions, and systems such as the International Classification of Diseases (ICD-10-CM), Current Procedural Terminology (CPT), and the Healthcare Common Procedure Coding System (HCPCS). Developing a solid foundation in these coding systems is essential for your success as a CPC.

- **Anatomy and Physiology Knowledge:** A thorough understanding of anatomy and physiology is vital for accurately assigning medical codes. This knowledge will help you interpret medical documentation, identify relevant diagnoses and procedures, and ensure the codes you post accurately reflect the patient's condition and treatment.

- **Medical Terminology:** Familiarity with medical terminology is essential for interpreting medical records and understanding the language used by healthcare providers. As a CPC, you should be able to recognize and understand commonly used medical terms, abbreviations, and acronyms.

- **Attention to Detail:** Medical coding requires high accuracy and precision; even minor errors can have significant financial and legal consequences. As a CPC, you must be meticulous and double-check your coding assignments to ensure their accuracy and completeness.

- **Critical Thinking and Problem-Solving:** Medical coding often involves complex cases that require careful analysis and interpretation. As a CPC, you must apply critical thinking and problem-solving skills to decipher medical documentation, identify inconsistencies, and assign the most appropriate codes.

- **Time Management and Organization:** Medical coders often work under tight deadlines and may need to manage multiple tasks simultaneously. Effective time management and organizational skills are crucial for consistently staying on top of your workload and meeting deadlines.

- **Adaptability and Flexibility:** The healthcare industry continuously evolves, with frequent updates to coding guidelines, regulations, and technology. As a CPC, you must be adaptable and flexible, able to adjust to new information and changes in the industry quickly.

- **Communication Skills:** Strong communication skills are essential for working effectively with colleagues, healthcare providers, and other professionals in the medical coding field. As a CPC, you need to be able to clearly explain your coding decisions, ask for clarification when needed, and collaborate with others to ensure accurate and efficient coding processes.

- **Computer Skills:** As a CPC, you'll rely on software programs and electronic health record (EHR) systems to access patient information, enter codes, and generate reports. Proficiency in using computers and relevant software is crucial for efficiently managing your daily tasks.

- **Integrity and Ethical Conduct:** Medical coders must adhere to strict ethical guidelines and maintain high integrity in their work. As a CPC, you ensure accurate and compliant coding practices, protect patient confidentiality, and adhere to industry regulations.

- **Customer Service Orientation:** Medical coding professionals often interact with healthcare providers, billing departments, and insurance companies to resolve coding-related issues. As a CPC, you should be able to handle these interactions professionally and courteously, with a focus on providing excellent customer service and maintaining positive relationships.

- **Continuous Learning and Professional Development:** The ever-changing healthcare industry landscape requires CPCs to stay informed about industry developments and maintain their coding expertise. Committing to continuous learning and professional development will help you stay current with changes in the field and ensure your ongoing success as a CPC.

By developing and strengthening these essential skills and competencies, you'll be well-equipped to excel in your career as a Certified Professional Coder. Investing time and effort into honing these abilities will make you a more effective and efficient coder and open up opportunities for advancement and professional growth.

Specialization Opportunities

As a Certified Professional Coder (CPC), you possess a solid foundation in the ideas and methods of medical coding. However, due to the size of the healthcare industry, there are several opportunities to sharpen your abilities and increase your knowledge in specialized areas. Specialization can result in more specialized tasks, higher wages, and the ability to stand out on the job market. In this part, we'll examine some of the CPC specialty possibilities that are in high demand.

A person who codes treatments and diagnoses for patients not admitted to the hospital or gets care someplace other than an inpatient institution, such as a clinic, a doctor's office, or an emergency department, is known as an outpatient coder. The CPT, HCPCS Level II, and ICD-10-CM coding systems, as well as the particular rules and legislation that apply to outpatient services, must all be understood by a specialist in outpatient coding.

- **Inpatient coding specialist:** Classifying diagnoses and treatments for patients admitted to the hospital for treatment falls under the purview of inpatient coding. Inpatient coders must be proficient in the ICD-10-CM and ICD-10-PCS coding systems and the complex guidelines that govern inpatient coding, including the DRG system and the Medicare Severity-Diagnosis Related Group (MS-DRG) approach.

- **Specialist in Risk Adjustment Coding:** Accurate diagnostic data collection and reporting are the primary goals of this emerging area, which focuses on risk adjustment coding used to calculate patient risk scores. Insurance companies and government programs use these risk scores to decide how much to pay healthcare providers. Risk adjustment reasons call for specific coding standards and documentation requirements. Hence risk adjustment coders must be proficient in ICD-10-CM coding.

- **Specialist in interventional radiology coding:** Interventional radiology, a rapidly developing profession, uses cutting-edge imaging methods to direct minimally invasive surgical operations. An expert in interventional radiology coding needs to be well-versed in the CPT, ICD-10-CM, and HCPCS Level II coding systems and have a thorough understanding of anatomy, physiology, and the intricate procedures carried out in this field.

- **Specialist in oncology coding:** Oncology coding categorizes cancer-related diagnoses and treatments. The CPT, ICD-10-CM, and HCPCS Level II coding systems and a solid grounding in medical language, anatomy, and physiology are requirements for oncology coders, mainly as they apply to cancer diagnoses and therapies. Understanding the many cancer kinds, staging systems, and treatment regimens is necessary for this specialty, as are the specific coding and documentation standards for oncology treatments.

- **Pediatrics Coding Specialists:** Pediatrics coding specialists collaborate with medical professionals who treat kids of all ages, from infants to teenagers. This specialization necessitates proficiency in the CPT, ICD-10-CM, and HCPCS Level II coding systems and a complete awareness of the particular coding and documentation standards for pediatric services. Coders must be informed about typical pediatric illnesses, developmental milestones, and age-specific diagnostic and therapeutic protocols.

- **Specialist in cardiology coding:** Cardiology coding entails categorizing diagnoses and treatments connected to the cardiovascular system. The CPT, ICD-10-CM, and HCPCS Level II coding systems, as well as a thorough knowledge of the anatomy and physiology of the heart and circulatory system, are requirements for cardiology coders. Understanding different heart diseases, diagnostic procedures, available therapies, and the particular coding and documentation standards for cardiology services are prerequisites for this specialty.

- **Specialist in orthopedic coding:** Coders in orthopedics are responsible for classifying diagnoses and treatments regarding the musculoskeletal system, which includes the bones, joints, muscles, and connective tissues. It is essential to thoroughly understand the medical terminology, anatomy, and physiology of the musculoskeletal system, CPT, ICD-10-CM, and HCPCS Level II coding systems as they relate to the orthopedic system. Additionally, this specialization will require knowledge of the specific coding and documentation requirements for orthopedic therapies and an understanding of a wide range of orthopedic illnesses, procedures, and treatment options.

- In obstetrics and gynecology, specialists in coding work alongside doctors who treat female patients during and after their reproductive years. This specialty must be familiar with the unique coding and documentation requirements for obstetrics and gynecology services, which require proficiency in the CPT, ICD-10-CM, and HCPCS Level II coding systems. Coders for obstetrics and gynecology must be familiar with common ailments, diagnostic techniques, and treatments for women's health in addition to pregnancy, labor, and postpartum care.

- **Specialist in emergency department coding:** Classifying diagnoses and treatments for patients who get care in an emergency room environment is called emergency department coding. Emergency department coders must master CPT, ICD-10-CM, and HCPCS Level II coding systems, and they also need to be well-versed in the particular regulations that pertain to emergency services. This specialty necessitates familiarity with various emergencies, diagnostic procedures, and therapeutic alternatives and the capacity to function successfully under time constraints.

- **Specialist in Evaluation and Management (E/M) Coding:** E/M coding is concerned with categorizing the evaluation and management services that medical practitioners offer to patients. E/M coders must be proficient in the CPT and ICD-10-CM coding systems and be thoroughly aware of these services' particular standards and documentation needs. Understanding the many E/M service levels, as well as the essential elements and determining variables that affect which level of service is most appropriate, is necessary for this specialty.

These are only a handful of the numerous specialization options open to CPCs. It's critical to assess your interests, strengths, and career objectives as you decide which path to take. Although pursuing a specialty could necessitate more education, experience, or training, the reward could be more advanced jobs, more professional satisfaction, and higher income potential. You can have a prosperous and fulfilling career as a specialized medical coder by keeping up with market developments and consistently enhancing your knowledge and abilities.

Successful Career Paths for Certified Professional Coders

The opportunity for a fruitful and rewarding career as a Certified Professional Coder (CPC) is enormous. Several options are available to you, each with its potential for advancement as a professional. In this section, we'll talk about some of the most well-liked and lucrative career opportunities for CPCs.

- **Medical Coding Specialist:** The most prevalent path for CPCs to start their careers is as a medical coding specialist. You will be in charge of appropriately assigning codes to diagnoses, procedures, and services listed inpatient medical records while doing this job function. This entry-level position offers the necessary training and experience for more advanced responsibilities, making it a good starting point for a career in medical coding.

- **Medical Coding Auditor:** As your knowledge and proficiency in medical coding increase, consider pursuing a job in this field. Auditors examine and analyze medical records, coding assignments, and documentation to verify accuracy, completeness, and conformity with coding standards and laws. Medical coding inspectors also offer input to help coders and other healthcare professionals improve the caliber of coding and documentation procedures.

- **Trainer/Educator in Coding:** If you appreciate coaching and educating others, becoming a trainer or educator in coding may be the ideal option for you. Coding educators create and present training courses, seminars, and workshops on various coding-related subjects, such as revisions to coding standards, legal requirements, and best practices in medical coding. Strong communication and presentation abilities and an in-depth understanding of medical coding principles and regulations are often needed for this position.

- **Medical Coding Manager/Supervisor:** You could be prepared to take on a management or supervisory job in medical coding if you have the required skills and a record of accomplishment. You will oversee a team of medical coders in this position, ensuring their work is precise and efficient while providing guidance and support to help them progress in their careers. Medical coding managers collaborate closely with other healthcare professionals, including physicians, nurses, and administrators, to develop and execute coding guidelines and procedures that improve the overall quality of treatment and patient outcomes.

- **Compliance Officer:** As a CPC with knowledge of medical coding standards and laws, you can consider pursuing a compliance career. Compliance officers are responsible for developing, implementing, and maintaining policies and procedures that guarantee an organization's conformance to national, state, and sector-specific legislation. The ability to successfully explain complicated material to numerous stakeholders and a thorough awareness of coding standards and regulations are requirements for this position.

- **Revenue Cycle Manager:** Working as a revenue cycle manager can be a rewarding career choice for CPCs. This position entails managing every step of the revenue cycle, from insurance verification and patient registration to billing, collections, and payment posting. Revenue cycle managers must have a thorough awareness of medical coding and billing procedures and have exceptional organizational and management abilities to ensure that healthcare organizations are paid accurately and quickly for the services they offer.

- **Health Information Manager:** A profession in health information management (HIM) is an option for CPCs. Health information managers are in charge of their collection, storage, and retrieval to ensure the accuracy, security, and privacy of patient medical records. This position frequently calls for understanding electronic health record (EHR) systems, health information technology, data analysis, and medical coding experience.

These are just a handful of the numerous lucrative employment possibilities open to CPCs. It's crucial to keep learning new things as you advance in your job, stay current on market developments, and be open to further personal and professional growth opportunities. You can build a successful and fulfilling career in the dynamic world of medical coding by staying adaptable and proactive.

Practice Test

Surgery

1. A patient undergoes a laparoscopic cholecystectomy due to chronic cholecystitis. The surgeon accidentally nicks the common bile duct during the procedure, resulting in a minor leak. The surgeon repairs the chimney immediately. How should the repair be coded?
   A. As an integral part of the cholecystectomy
   B. As a separate procedure with a distinct code
   C. As an unlisted procedure in the surgery section
   D. As an additional cholecystectomy procedure

2. A patient with a history of gastric bypass surgery presents with recurrent abdominal pain. The surgeon identifies and removes a bezoar from the gastric pouch during an exploratory laparotomy. How should the bezoar removal be coded?
   A. As a foreign body removal
   B. As a gastrostomy revision
   C. As a gastrotomy with the removal of the bezoar
   D. As a gastroplasty revision

3. Which of the following is the correct Code for an open, total, unilateral inguinal hernia repair using mesh in a 45-year-old male?
   A. 49505
   B. 49507
   C. 49520
   D. 49525

4. A patient undergoes a sigmoid colectomy for diverticulitis. The surgeon performs a primary anastomosis and does not create a colostomy. How should the procedure be coded?
   A. 44140
   B. 44141
   C. 44143
   D. 44144

5. A 12-year-old patient with acute appendicitis undergoes an open appendectomy. During the procedure, the surgeon encounters a gangrenous appendix that has perforated. What modifier should be appended to the Code for the appendectomy?
   A. -22
   B. -51
   C. -52
   D. -59

6. Which of the following codes is used to report a diagnostic laparoscopy for a patient with a suspected intra-abdominal mass?
   A. 49320
   B. 49321
   C. 49322
   D. 49323

7. A surgeon performs a laparoscopic Nissen fundoplication to treat gastroesophageal reflux disease (GERD) patient. What is the correct Code for this procedure?
   A. 43279
   B. 43280
   C. 43281
   D. 43282

8. A patient undergoes an open cholecystectomy with intraoperative cholangiography. The cholangiography reveals a stone in the common bile duct. The surgeon then performs a choledochotomy to remove the stone. How should the choledochotomy be coded?
   A. 47480
   B. 47562
   C. 47600
   D. 47605

9. What Code is used to report the excision of a pilonidal cyst using a rhomboid flap technique?
   A. 11770
   B. 11771
   C. 11772
   D. 11774

10. A patient with a history of recurrent femoral hernias undergoes a bilateral open femoral hernia repair using mesh. Which of the following codes would be used for this procedure?
    A. 49550
    B. 49553
    C. 49555
    D. 49557

11. Which of the following codes is used to report a laparoscopic repair of a recurrent ventral hernia with mesh?
    A. 49560
    B. 49561
    C. 49565
    D. 49566

12. A surgeon performs an excisional biopsy on a patient with a suspicious breast mass. Postoperative pathology reveals that the group is malignant. The surgeon then schedules a modified radical mastectomy. How should the excisional biopsy be coded?
    A. 19120
    B. 19125
    C. 19126
    D. 19130

13. A patient with a known history of Crohn's disease undergoes an ileocolic resection. The surgeon performs a side-to-side anastomosis to restore bowel continuity. Which Code should be used for this procedure?
    A. 44160
    B. 44187
    C. 44204
    D. 44205

14. A patient undergoes an elective laparoscopic splenectomy due to hypersplenism. The surgeon encounters significant adhesions during the procedure and decides to convert to an open splenectomy. How should the open splenectomy be coded?
    A. 38100
    B. 38101
    C. 38115
    D. 38120

15. A patient diagnosed with a malignant neoplasm of the colon undergoes a right hemicolectomy with an ileocolic anastomosis. What is the correct Code for this procedure?
    A. 44140
    B. 44145
    C. 44150
    D. 44160

16. A patient with a diagnosis of rectal prolapse undergoes a laparoscopic rectopexy. What is the correct Code for this procedure?
    A. 45540
    B. 45541
    C. 45550
    D. 45560

17. A surgeon performs laparoscopic lysis of adhesions in a patient with a history of multiple abdominal surgeries. Which Code should be used for this procedure?
    A. 44005
    B. 44180
    C. 44200
    D. 44201

18. What is the correct Code for an open repair of a recurrent umbilical hernia without mesh?
    A. 49580
    B. 49581
    C. 49582
    D. 49585

19. A patient with a diagnosis of anal fistula undergoes a fistulotomy. What is the appropriate Code for this procedure?
    A. 46020
    B. 46030
    C. 46040
    D. 46050

20. A surgeon performs a total abdominal hysterectomy with bilateral salpingo-oophorectomy for a patient with a malignant ovarian tumor. How should this procedure be coded?
    A. 58940
    B. 58943
    C. 58950
    D. 58951

21. A patient undergoes an exploratory laparotomy with lysis of adhesions and a partial colectomy with anastomosis for a bowel obstruction. How should this procedure be coded?
    A. 44020
    B. 44120
    C. 44121
    D. 44125

22. What is the appropriate Code for an open incision and drainage of a perirectal abscess?
    A. 46030
    B. 46040
    C. 46050
    D. 46060

23. Which of the following codes is used to report a laparoscopic repair of a diaphragmatic hernia with mesh?
   A. 39530
   B. 39531
   C. 39540
   D. 39545

24. A patient undergoes a laparoscopic gastric band adjustment without imaging guidance. What is the correct Code for this procedure?
   A. 43770
   B. 43771
   C. 43773
   D. 43774

25. A patient with a history of cholecystectomy presents with abdominal pain. A surgeon performs a laparoscopic exploration of the common bile duct and finds a retained stone, which is then removed. What is the appropriate Code for this procedure?
   A. 47531
   B. 47532
   C. 47533
   D. 47534

26. A surgeon performs a laparoscopic Roux-en-Y gastric bypass for a patient with morbid obesity. What is the correct Code for this procedure?
   A. 43644
   B. 43645
   C. 43659
   D. 43770

27. What is the appropriate Code for an excision of a subcutaneous soft tissue tumor from the abdominal wall?
   A. 22900
   B. 22901
   C. 22902
   D. 22903

28. A patient undergoes a laparoscopic sleeve gastrectomy for morbid obesity. What is the correct Code for this procedure?
   A. 43775
   B. 43776
   C. 43777
   D. 43778

29. A surgeon performs an open liver biopsy for a patient with a suspected hepatic lesion. What is the appropriate Code for this procedure?
   A. 47000
   B. 47001
   C. 47100
   D. 47120

30. A patient diagnosed with colon cancer undergoes a laparoscopic-assisted sigmoid colectomy with anastomosis. What is the correct Code for this procedure?
   A. 44206
   B. 44207
   C. 44208
   D. 44210

31. A surgeon performs an open excision of a submucosal lesion in the stomach. What is the appropriate Code for this procedure?
   A. 43620
   B. 43621
   C. 43622
   D. 43623

32. A patient undergoes an open excision of Meckel's diverticulum. What is the correct Code for this procedure?
   A. 44180
   B. 44186
   C. 44200
   D. 44202

33. A patient diagnosed with varicose veins undergoes a radiofrequency ablation of the great saphenous vein. What is the appropriate Code for this procedure?
   A. 36475
   B. 36478
   C. 36479
   D. 36482

34. A patient undergoes a laparoscopic left adrenalectomy for a benign tumor. What is the correct Code for this procedure?
   A. 60540
   B. 60545
   C. 60650
   D. 60659

35. A patient diagnosed with morbid obesity undergoes a laparoscopic adjustable gastric banding. What is the appropriate Code for this procedure?
   A. 43770
   B. 43772
   C. 43773
   D. 43774

36. A patient undergoes a laparoscopic repair of a recurrent inguinal hernia with mesh. What is the correct Code for this procedure?
   A. 49650
   B. 49651
   C. 49652
   D. 49653

Evaluation and Management

1. A patient presents to the primary care clinic with sinus infection symptoms. The physician takes a detailed history, performs a problem-focused examination, and prescribes an antibiotic. What critical component of evaluation and management is demonstrated in this scenario?
   A. Medical decision-making
   B. time spent with the patient
   C. Coordination of care
   D. Counseling

2. What does the term "level of service" refer to in evaluating and management?
   A. The complexity of the patient's condition
   B. The amount of time spent with the patient
   C. The type and extent of the service provided
   D. The reimbursement rate for the service

3. A patient visits their primary care physician for the management of hypertension. The physician spends 25 minutes discussing diet, exercise, and medication adjustments. According to the guidelines for evaluation and management, what factor can be considered when selecting the appropriate Code for this visit?
   A. The severity of the patient's condition
   B. The physician's level of expertise
   C. The amount of time spent counseling the patient
   D. The need for a referral to a specialist

4. When selecting the appropriate evaluation and management code for a patient encounter, which three key components should be considered?
   A. History, examination, and medical decision-making
   B. Time spent, coordination of care, and counseling
   C. Patient demographics, diagnosis, and treatment plan
   D. Severity of the patient's condition, physician expertise, and location of service

5. What is the purpose of a consultation code in the context of evaluation and management services?
   A. To bill for services provided by a specialist at the request of another provider
   B. To bill for a second opinion on a complex case
   C. To bill for ongoing management of a chronic condition
   D. To bill for a follow-up visit after a procedure

6. In evaluating and managing services, what is the primary difference between a new and established patient?
   A. The length of time since the patient's last visit
   B. The patient's age and medical history
   C. The reason for the patient's visit
   D. The complexity of the patient's condition

Anesthesia

1. Which factors determine the appropriate anesthesia code for a surgical procedure?
   A. The surgeon's years of experience
   B. The type of anesthesia used
   C. The patient's age
   D. The patient's overall health status

2. In the context of anesthesia coding, what is the purpose of the anesthesia base unit?
   A. To determine the total time spent administering anesthesia
   B. To account for the complexity of the anesthesia service provided
   C. To calculate the number of additional units for medical direction
   D. To identify the specific anesthesia procedure performed

3. What should be considered in addition to the base units for the anesthesia code when coding anesthesia services?
   A. The number of surgical assistants
   B. The specific surgical instruments used
   C. The amount of time the anesthesiologist spends with the patient
   D. The type of medication administered during the procedure

4. What does the term "medical direction" refer to for anesthesia services?
   A. The supervision of a certified registered nurse anesthetist (CRNA) by an anesthesiologist
   B. The anesthesiologist's instructions to the surgical team during the procedure
   C. The specific anesthesia technique used during the surgery
   D. The documentation provided by the anesthesiologist for billing purposes

Radiology

1. What is the purpose of a diagnostic radiology report?
   A. To provide a detailed description of the radiology procedure
   B. To offer a comprehensive analysis of the patient's medical history
   C. To present the radiologist's interpretation of the imaging study
   D. To document the type of anesthesia used during the procedure

2. What is the primary factor determining the appropriate CPT code when coding for radiology services?
   A. The type of radiology equipment used
   B. The body part or organ system examined
   C. The patient's age and gender
   D. The radiologist's years of experience

3. Which of the following imaging modalities uses sound waves to create images of the body's internal structures?
   A. Magnetic Resonance Imaging (MRI)
   B. Computed Tomography (CT)
   C. Ultrasound
   D. Positron Emission Tomography (PET)

4. In radiology coding, what is the difference between professional and technical components?
   A. The professional component refers to the radiologist's interpretation, while the technical part covers the cost of equipment and staff
   B. The professional component covers the cost of equipment and staff, while the technical part refers to the radiologist's interpretation
   C. The professional component pertains to the radiology procedure, while the technical part covers the cost of the imaging study
   D. The professional component pertains to the type of anesthesia used, while the technical segment covers the cost of the imaging study

5. What is the primary purpose of a contrast agent in radiology?
   A. To decrease patient discomfort during the procedure
   B. To enhance the visibility of specific structures in the imaging study
   C. To reduce the radiation exposure to the patient
   D. To shorten the duration of the radiology procedure

6. What term describes the simultaneous performance of two or more radiology procedures on the same patient during the session?
   A. Stacking
   B. Bundling
   C. Overlapping
   D. Concurrent

Laboratory/Pathology

1. A patient with a history of iron-deficiency anemia undergoes a laboratory test to determine their complete blood count (CBC). Which components would be most relevant to assessing the patient's anemia status?
    A. Hemoglobin level
    B. White blood cell count
    C. Platelet count
    D. Erythrocyte sedimentation rate

2. A physician orders a blood test for a patient suspected of having a bacterial infection. Which of the following laboratory tests would be most helpful in confirming the presence of a bacterial infection?
    A. C-reactive protein (CRP)
    B. Basic metabolic panel (BMP)
    C. Prothrombin time (PT)
    D. Partial thromboplastin time (PTT)

3. A patient presents with fatigue, weight gain, and cold intolerance symptoms. The physician suspects hypothyroidism and orders a laboratory test to assess thyroid function. Which of the following tests would be most appropriate to evaluate the patient's thyroid function?
    A. Thyroid-stimulating hormone (TSH)
    B. Triiodothyronine (T3)
    C. Thyroxine (T4)
    D. Thyroglobulin

4. A patient with a history of liver disease undergoes laboratory testing to evaluate their liver function. Which of the following tests is a critical component of a comprehensive liver function panel?
    A. Alanine aminotransferase (ALT)
    B. Creatinine
    C. Blood urea nitrogen (BUN)
    D. Lactate dehydrogenase (LDH)

5. A patient presents with symptoms of joint pain and stiffness. The physician suspects rheumatoid arthritis and orders a laboratory test to help confirm the diagnosis. Which of the following tests would be most appropriate in this case?
    A. Rheumatoid factor (RF)
    B. Antinuclear antibody (ANA)
    C. Cyclic citrullinated peptide (CCP)
    D. Erythrocyte sedimentation rate (ESR)

6. A patient with a family history of colorectal cancer undergoes a laboratory test to screen for early signs of the disease. Which of the following tests is commonly used as a non-invasive screening tool for colorectal cancer?
    A. Fecal immunochemical test (FIT)
    B. Carcinoembryonic antigen (CEA)
    C. Alpha-fetoprotein (AFP)
    D. Prostate-specific antigen (PSA)

Medicine

1. A patient presents with fatigue, shortness of breath, and pallor. The physician suspects anemia and orders laboratory tests. Which of the following tests would be the most appropriate initial test to confirm the diagnosis of anemia?
   A. Hemoglobin (Hgb)
   B. Hematocrit (Hct)
   C. Reticulocyte count
   D. Iron studies

2. A patient with a history of hypertension is prescribed medication to help lower blood pressure. Which of the following medicines is commonly used as a first-line treatment for hypertension?
   A. Calcium channel blockers (CCBs)
   B. Beta-blockers (BBs)
   C. Angiotensin-converting enzyme (ACE) inhibitors
   D. Diuretics

3. A 65-year-old patient presents with a productive cough, fever, and shortness of breath. The physician suspects pneumonia and orders a diagnostic test to confirm the diagnosis. Which of the following tests is typically used to diagnose pneumonia?
   A. Chest X-ray
   B. Sputum culture
   C. Complete blood count (CBC)
   D. Bronchoscopy

4. A patient presents with symptoms of hyperthyroidism, such as weight loss, tremors, and increased heart rate. Which of the following laboratory tests is commonly used to evaluate thyroid function and diagnose hyperthyroidism?
   A. Thyroid-stimulating hormone (TSH)
   B. Free thyroxine (T4)
   C. Total triiodothyronine (T3)
   D. Thyroid peroxidase antibody (TPOAb)

5. A patient with a history of type 2 diabetes is scheduled for a routine check-up. Which of the following tests is commonly used to monitor long-term blood sugar control in diabetic patients?
   A. Fasting plasma glucose (FPG)
   B. Oral glucose tolerance test (OGTT)
   C. Hemoglobin A1c (HbA1c)
   D. Random plasma glucose (RPG)

6. A patient is prescribed a medication to lower cholesterol levels. Which medications are commonly used as a first-line treatment for hyperlipidemia?
   A. Statins
   B. Fibrates
   C. Niacin
   D. Bile acid sequestrants

Medical Terminology

1. The term "dyspnea" refers to which of the following symptoms?
   A. Difficulty swallowing
   B. Rapid heartbeat
   C. Difficulty breathing
   D. Chest pain

2. The medical term "myocardial infarction" refers to which of the following conditions?
   A. Stroke
   B. Heart attack
   C. Heart failure
   D. Angina

3. The term "nephrolithiasis" describes the presence of what in the kidneys?
   A. Infection
   B. Cysts
   C. Stones
   D. Tumors

4. The medical term "arthralgia" refers to which of the following symptoms?
   A. Joint pain
   B. Muscle weakness
   C. Nerve pain
   D. Bone fracture

Anatomy

1. Which of the following structures is responsible for cerebrospinal fluid (CSF) production in the brain?
   A. Choroid plexus
   B. Arachnoid granulations
   C. Cerebral cortex
   D. Pineal gland

2. The primary function of the large intestine is to:
   A. Digest proteins
   B. Absorb nutrients
   C. Produce bile
   D. Reabsorb water and electrolytes

3. The bones of the human wrist, also known as the carpal bones, are categorized into how many rows?
   A. One
   B. Two
   C. Three
   D. Four

4. Which of the following muscles is responsible for flexion and medial rotation of the hip joint?
   A. Biceps femoris
   B. Gluteus maximus
   C. Iliopsoas
   D. Sartorius

ICD-10-CM

1. Which ICD-10-CM codes would be used for patients diagnosed with essential (primary) hypertension?
   A. I10
   B. I11
   C. I12
   D. I15

2. In ICD-10-CM, what character is used as a placeholder for codes that require a seventh character but do not have a sixth character?
   A. X
   B. Y
   C. Z
   D. 0

3. A patient is diagnosed with type 2 diabetes mellitus with diabetic neuropathy. What is the correct ICD-10-CM code for this condition?
   A. E10.40
   B. E10.41
   C. E11.40
   D. E11.41

4. Which ICD-10-CM codes would be used to report acute bronchitis due to the respiratory syncytial virus (RSV)?
   A. J20.5
   B. J20.6
   C. J20.7
   D. J20.8

5. In ICD-10-CM, what is the correct Code for a patient diagnosed with moderate, nonproliferative diabetic retinopathy without macular edema, in the right eye, due to type 2 diabetes mellitus?
   A. E11.331
   B. E11.339
   C. E11.341
   D. E11.349

HCPCS Level II

1. Which of the following HCPCS Level II codes is used for reporting the administration of the seasonal influenza vaccine?
   A. G0008
   B. G0009
   C. G0010
   D. 90471

2. What is the appropriate HCPCS Level II code for a standard manual wheelchair?
   A. E0978
   B. E0981
   C. E0985
   D. K0001

3. Which of the following HCPCS Level II codes is used to report an injection of 10 units of onabotulinumtoxinA (Botox)?
   A. J0585
   B. J0586
   C. J0587
   D. J0588

Coding Guidelines

1. According to ICD-10-CM coding guidelines, what should a coder do when a patient has an acute and chronic condition, and different codes are available for each?
   A. Code only the acute condition
   B. Code only the chronic condition
   C. Code both the acute and chronic conditions
   D. Code neither condition, as it would be redundant

2. When a patient is admitted for the sole purpose of receiving chemotherapy, what is the appropriate principal diagnosis code?
   A. The Code for the Malignancy
   B. The Code for the Encounter for Chemotherapy
   C. The Code for the chemotherapy drug administered
   D. The Code for the side effect or complication, if present

3. According to CPT coding guidelines, what should a coder do when a procedure is performed bilaterally?
   A. Use the Code for the unilateral procedure
   B. Use the Code for the bilateral procedure
   C. Use the unilateral procedure code with a -50 modifier
   D. Use the bilateral procedure code with a -51 modifier

4. In ICD-10-CM, what is the purpose of an Excludes1 note?
   A. To indicate that two codes cannot be reported together
   B. To provide further information about the Code
   C. To list alternative codes for the same condition
   D. To indicate that the condition represented by the Code is part of a more significant condition

5. When coding for injuries, which of the following is the correct order for coding according to ICD-10-CM guidelines?
   A. Primary injury, secondary injury, external cause
   B. External cause, primary injury, secondary injury
   C. Primary injury, external cause, secondary injury
   D. Secondary injury, primary injury, external cause

6. According to CPT coding guidelines, what is the appropriate way to code for multiple procedures performed during the same surgical session?
   A. Code only the most complex procedure
   B. Code all procedures and append modifier -51 to the secondary procedure(s)
   C. Code all procedures and append modifier -59 to the secondary procedure(s)
   D. Code all procedures and append modifier -22 to the secondary procedure(s)

7. What is the correct way to code a diagnosis that is documented as "probable" or "suspected" in an outpatient setting, according to ICD-10-CM coding guidelines?
   A. Code the probable or suspected diagnosis
   B. Code the signs and symptoms related to the probable or suspected diagnosis
   C. Code the most likely alternative diagnosis
   D. Code the condition as if it were confirmed

Compliance and Regulatory

1. Which of the following is a critical component of a medical practice's compliance plan, according to the Office of Inspector General (OIG)?
    A. Requiring employees to memorize all regulations
    B. Designating a compliance officer or contact
    C. Having a single, unchangeable compliance plan
    D. Ignoring potential violations until they become critical

2. Under HIPAA regulations, a covered entity must provide patients access to their medical records within what timeframe?
    A. 5 days
    B. 15 days
    C. 30 days
    D. 60 days

3. The Stark Law prohibits physicians from making referrals for specific services payable by Medicare to an entity with which the physician or their immediate family member has a financial relationship unless a particular exception applies. Which of the following services is NOT subject to the Stark Law?
    A. Physical therapy services
    B. Radiology services
    C. Clinical laboratory services
    D. Routine wellness exams

Cases

1. A patient visits a primary care physician complaining of fatigue, weight loss, and frequent urination. The physician orders blood tests and diagnoses the patient with type 2 diabetes. The physician prescribes medication, provides dietary advice, and schedules a follow-up appointment.

2. A patient undergoes a total knee replacement due to severe osteoarthritis. The surgery is successful, but the patient develops a postoperative infection. The surgeon prescribes antibiotics and schedules a follow-up appointment.

3. A patient presents to the emergency department with chest pain and shortness of breath. The physician orders an electrocardiogram (EKG) and lab work. The results indicate the patient has a myocardial infarction (heart attack). The patient is admitted for further treatment and management.

4. A pediatric patient is seen for a well-child visit. The patient's growth and development are within normal limits. The physician administers routine vaccinations and schedules a follow-up appointment in one year.

5. A patient presents to a dermatologist with a suspicious skin lesion. The dermatologist performs a punch biopsy and sends the sample for pathology testing. The results reveal a basal cell carcinoma. The dermatologist schedules a follow-up appointment to discuss treatment options.

6. A patient undergoes an elective hernia repair surgery. The surgery is booming, and the patient is discharged the same day with instructions for postoperative care and a prescription for pain medication.

7. A patient is referred to a gastroenterologist for a colonoscopy due to a family history of colon cancer. The gastroenterologist performs the colonoscopy and removes several polyps for biopsy. The pathology results reveal benign adenomatous polyps.

8. A patient visits a psychiatrist for symptoms of depression and anxiety. The psychiatrist conducts a thorough evaluation, diagnoses the patient with major depressive disorder and generalized anxiety disorder, and prescribes medication. The psychiatrist also schedules a follow-up appointment for therapy and medication management.

9. A patient visits an allergist due to seasonal allergies. The allergist performs skin testing to determine the specific allergens causing the patient's symptoms. Based on the test results, the allergist prescribes allergy medication and recommends immunotherapy.

10. A patient visits a cardiologist for a routine follow-up appointment after a previous myocardial infarction. The cardiologist reviews the patient's medical history, performs a physical examination, and orders a stress test to evaluate the patient's heart function. The stress test results show no significant changes, and the patient is advised to continue with their current treatment plan.

Ethical and Legal Considerations

1. Which of the following is an example of a potential breach of patient confidentiality?
   A. Discussing a patient's medical condition with their family members without consent
   B. Obtaining informed consent before surgery
   C. Reporting suspected child abuse to the appropriate authorities
   D. Informing a patient of their diagnosis and treatment options

2. What is the main purpose of the Health Insurance Portability and Accountability Act (HIPAA)?
   A. To ensure fair pricing for medical services
   B. To protect patient privacy and ensure the security of health information
   C. To regulate health insurance policies and coverage
   D. To establish guidelines for medical education and training

3. Which of the following is an ethical consideration when coding medical records?
   A. Assigning codes based on the highest level of reimbursement
   B. Reporting only accurate and complete codes based on documentation
   C. Assigning codes to make the patient's condition seem more severe
   D. Ignoring discrepancies in the medical documentation

4. What is the primary role of a medical coder in the context of healthcare fraud and abuse prevention?
   A. Investigating potential fraud cases
   B. Ensuring accurate and compliant coding and billing practices
   C. Reporting colleagues who engage in unethical behavior
   D. Advising patients on their rights and responsibilities

5. A patient refuses a recommended treatment due to personal beliefs. What should a healthcare provider do in this situation?
   A. Respect the patient's autonomy and explore alternative treatment options
   B. Insist on the recommended treatment and disregard the patient's preferences
   C. Report the patient to the medical board for non-compliance
   D. Refuse to treat the patient further

6. Which of the following is an example of a potential conflict of interest in a medical setting?
   A. A physician receives financial incentives for prescribing a specific medication
   B. A nurse provides care for a family member
   C. A medical coder is responsible for coding their own medical records
   D. A surgeon performs surgery on a close friend

7. What is the main purpose of the False Claims Act?
   A. To regulate the marketing of prescription drugs
   B. To protect whistleblowers who report fraud
   C. To address healthcare fraud and abuse by penalizing the submission of false claims
   D. To establish guidelines for medical research

8. Informed consent is a legal and ethical requirement for which of the following medical interventions?
   A. Routine physical examination
   B. Blood pressure measurement
   C. Vaccination
   D. Major surgery

9. What is the most appropriate action for a medical coder to take if they suspect fraudulent coding or billing practices in their workplace?
    A. Report their concerns to a supervisor or compliance officer
    B. Confront the person responsible for the suspected fraud directly
    C. Ignore the issue and continue their work as usual
    D. Report the issue to the media

10. What is the primary goal of medical ethics?
    A. To establish guidelines for fair reimbursement of medical services
    B. To protect the rights and interests of healthcare providers
    C. To ensure that medical decisions are made in the best interest of patients
    D. To promote the financial success of healthcare organizations

ANSWER KEY

Surgery Section

Answer: A. As an integral part of the cholecystectomy
Reason: Repairing the common bile duct is essential to cholecystectomy and would not be coded separately.

Answer: C. As a gastrotomy with the removal of the bezoar
Reason: Removing a bezoar from the gastric pouch should be coded as a gastrotomy (43770) with the removal of the bezoar, as it is not considered a foreign body removal or a revision of the gastric bypass.

Answer: B. 49507
Reason: Code 49507 is used for an open, total, unilateral inguinal hernia repair using mesh in a patient who is 18 or older.

Answer: C. 44143
Reason: Code 44143 is used for a colectomy with resection, with anastomosis for diverticulitis when no colostomy is created.

Answer: A. -22
Reason: Modifier -22 (Increased Procedural Services) should be appended to the Code for the appendectomy to indicate the increased complexity of the procedure due to the gangrenous, perforated appendix.

Answer: A. 49320
Reason: Code 49320 is used for a diagnostic laparoscopy to evaluate an intra-abdominal mass.

Answer: C. 43281
Reason: Code 43281 is used for a laparoscopic Nissen fundoplication to treat GERD.

Answer: B. 47562
Reason: Code 47562 is used for an open cholecystectomy with intraoperative cholangiography, with the addition of a choledochotomy to remove a stone from the common bile duct.

Answer: C. 11772
Reason: Code 11772 is used for the excision of a pilonidal cyst with a rhomboid flap technique.

Answer: D. 49557
Reason: Using mesh, code 49557 is used for a bilateral open femoral hernia repair.

Answer: D. 49566
Reason: Code 49566 is used for a laparoscopic repair of a recurrent ventral hernia with mesh.

Answer: B. 19125
Reason: Code 19125 is used for an excisional biopsy of a breast lesion with the lesion identified as malignant postoperatively.

Answer: A. 44160
Reason: Code 44160 is used for an ileocolic resection with a side-to-side anastomosis for a patient with Crohn's disease.

Answer: A. 38100
Reason: Code 38100 is used for an open splenectomy, converted from a laparoscopic splenectomy due to significant adhesions.

Answer: A. 44140
Reason: Code 44140 is used for a right hemicolectomy with an ileocolic anastomosis in a patient with a malignant neoplasm of the colon.

Answer: B. 45541
Reason: 45541 is the specific Code for laparoscopic rectopexy.

Answer: B. 44180
Reason: 44180 is the Code for laparoscopic lysis of adhesions.

Answer: B. 49581
Reason: 49581 represents the open repair of a recurrent umbilical hernia without mesh.

Answer: B. 46030
Reason: 46030 is the Code for a fistulotomy for an anal fistula.

Answer: B. 58943
Reason: 58943 is the Code for a total abdominal hysterectomy with bilateral salpingo-oophorectomy for a malignant ovarian tumor.

Answer: C. 44121
Reason: 44121 is the Code for partial colectomy with anastomosis, and the exploratory laparotomy and lysis of adhesions are included.

Answer: D. 46060
Reason: 46060 is the Code for open incision and drainage of a perirectal abscess.

Answer: B. 39531
Reason: 39531 is the Code for laparoscopic repair of diaphragmatic hernia with mesh.

Answer: C. 43773
Reason: 43773 is the laparoscopic gastric band adjustment code without imaging guidance.

Answer: B. 47532
Reason: 47532 is the Code for laparoscopic exploration and removal of a retained stone in the common bile duct.

Answer: A. 43644
Reason: 43644 is the Code for a laparoscopic Roux-en-Y gastric bypass.

Answer: A. 22900
Reason: 22900 is the Code for the excision of a subcutaneous soft tissue tumor from the abdominal wall.

Answer: A. 43775
Reason: 43775 is the Code for laparoscopic sleeve gastrectomy.

Answer: A. 47000
Reason: 47000 is the Code for an open liver biopsy.

Answer: A. 44206
Reason: 44206 is the Code for laparoscopic-assisted sigmoid colectomy with anastomosis.

Answer: C. 43622
Reason: 43622 is the Code for open excision of a submucosal lesion in the stomach.

Answer: A. 44180
Reason: 44180 is the Code for open excision of Meckel's diverticulum.

Answer: A. 36475
Reason: 36475 is the Code for radiofrequency ablation of the great saphenous vein.

Answer: C. 60650
Reason: 60650 is the Code for laparoscopic left adrenalectomy for a benign tumor.

Answer: B. 43772
Reason: 43772 is the Code for laparoscopic adjustable gastric banding.

Answer: A. 49650
Reason: 49650 is the Code for laparoscopic repair of a recurrent inguinal hernia with mesh.

Evaluation and Management

Answer: A. Medical decision-making
Reason: The physician assesses the patient's symptoms, makes a diagnosis, and prescribes treatment, demonstrating the medical decision-making component of evaluation and management.

Answer: C. The type and extent of the service provided
Reason: The level of service refers to the complexity and time of the evaluation and management service provided to the patient, which is used to determine the appropriate Code for billing purposes.

Answer: C. The amount of time spent counseling the patient
Reason: According to evaluation and management guidelines, the time spent counseling the patient can be considered when selecting the appropriate Code for a visit, as it may affect the level of service provided.

Answer: A. History, examination, and medical decision-making
Reason: These three key components are used to determine the appropriate evaluation and management code for a patient encounter, as they reflect the complexity and extent of the service provided.

Answer: A. To bill for services provided by a specialist at the request of another provider
Reason: Consultation codes are used for billing for evaluation and management services provided by a specialist at the request of another provider, usually to seek advice or guidance on managing a patient's condition.

Answer: A. The length of time since the patient's last visit
Reason: A new patient has not received professional services from a physician or a physician of the same specialty within the same practice group in the past three years. An established patient has received professional services from the physician or a physician of the same thing within the same practice group within the past three years.

Anesthesia

Answer: B. The type of anesthesia used
Reason: The type of anesthesia used for a surgical procedure is one factor that determines the appropriate anesthesia code, which considers the complexity of the service provided.

Answer: B. To account for the complexity of the anesthesia service provided
Reason: The anesthesia base unit is assigned to each anesthesia code to reflect the complexity of the anesthesia service provided for a specific surgical procedure.

Answer: C. The amount of time the anesthesiologist spends with the patient
Reason: In addition to the base units, anesthesia services are also coded based on the time units, representing the amount of time the anesthesiologist spends providing anesthesia care for the patient.

Answer: A. The supervision of a certified registered nurse anesthetist (CRNA) by an anesthesiologist
Reason: Medical direction refers to the supervision of a CRNA by an anesthesiologist during the provision of anesthesia services. Specific criteria must be met for the anesthesiologist to bill for medical direction.

Radiology

Answer: C. To present the radiologist's interpretation of the imaging study
Reason: The main purpose of a diagnostic radiology report is to provide the radiologist's interpretation of the imaging study, detailing their findings and conclusions based on the images.

Answer: B. The body part or organ system examined
Reason: The appropriate CPT code for radiology services is primarily determined by the body part or organ system being examined, as different codes correspond to different anatomical areas.

Answer: C. Ultrasound
Reason: Ultrasound is an imaging modality that utilizes sound waves to create images of the body's internal structures. MRI, CT, and PET scans use different methods to generate images.

Answer: A. The professional component refers to the radiologist's interpretation, while the technical part covers the cost of equipment and staff
Reason: In radiology coding, the professional component refers to the radiologist's interpretation of the imaging study, while the technical component includes the cost of the equipment and staff required for the procedure.

Answer: B. To enhance the visibility of specific structures in the imaging study
Reason: The primary purpose of a contrast agent in radiology is to improve the visibility of specific structures in the imaging study, helping the radiologist better visualize and analyze the area of interest.

Answer: D. Concurrent
Reason: The term "concurrent" describes the simultaneous performance of two or more radiology procedures on the same patient during the same session. The other terms listed do not accurately describe this situation.

Laboratory/Pathology

Answer: A. Hemoglobin level
Reason: Hemoglobin level is an essential component of the CBC test to assess a patient's anemia status, as it indicates the oxygen-carrying capacity of the red blood cells. Low hemoglobin levels are associated with iron-deficiency anemia.

Answer: A. C-reactive protein (CRP)
Reason: C-reactive protein (CRP) is an acute-phase reactant produced by the liver in response to inflammation, and its levels often rise during bacterial infections. A high CRP level can be indicative of a bacterial infection.

Answer: A. Thyroid-stimulating hormone (TSH)
Reason: Thyroid-stimulating hormone (TSH) is the most sensitive test for assessing thyroid function, as it is the primary regulator of thyroid hormone production. An elevated TSH level indicates hypothyroidism, while a low level suggests hyperthyroidism.

Answer: A. Alanine aminotransferase (ALT)
Reason: Alanine aminotransferase (ALT) is a vital component of a comprehensive liver function panel, as it is an enzyme found primarily in liver cells. Elevated ALT levels can indicate liver damage or disease.

Answer: C. Cyclic citrullinated peptide (CCP)
Reason: Cyclic citrullinated peptide (CCP) antibodies are particular for rheumatoid arthritis, and their presence in the blood is strongly associated with the disease. While rheumatoid factor (RF) and erythrocyte sedimentation rate (ESR) can also be elevated in rheumatoid arthritis, they are less specific and can be elevated in other conditions.

Answer: A. Fecal immunochemical test (FIT)
Reason: The fecal immunochemical test (FIT) is a non-invasive screening tool for colorectal cancer that detects the presence of hidden blood in the stool, which can be an early sign of the disease. Carcinoembryonic antigen (CEA), alpha-fetoprotein (AFP), and prostate-specific antigen (PSA) are tumor markers that can be elevated in various types of cancer but are not typically used for colorectal cancer screening.

Medicine

Answer: A. Hemoglobin (Hgb)
Reason: Hemoglobin (Hgb) is the most appropriate initial test to diagnose anemia, as it measures the amount of oxygen-carrying protein in the blood. Hematocrit (Hct), reticulocyte count, and iron studies may also be ordered but are not the initial test of choice.

Answer: C. Angiotensin-converting enzyme (ACE) inhibitors
Reason: ACE inhibitors are commonly used as a first-line treatment for hypertension, as they help relax blood vessels and lower blood pressure. Other medications, such as calcium channel blockers, beta-blockers, and diuretics, may also be used, but ACE inhibitors are often preferred initially.

Answer: A. Chest X-ray
Reason: A chest X-ray is typically used to diagnose pneumonia, as it can show the presence of an infection or inflammation in the lungs. Sputum culture, complete blood count (CBC), and bronchoscopy may also be used in the diagnostic process but are not the primary test of choice.

Answer: A. Thyroid-stimulating hormone (TSH)
Reason: Thyroid-stimulating hormone (TSH) is commonly used to evaluate thyroid function and diagnose hyperthyroidism, as it is the most sensitive test for detecting thyroid dysfunction. Free thyroxine (T4), total triiodothyronine (T3), and thyroid peroxidase antibody (TPOAb) may also be ordered, but TSH is the primary test of choice.

Answer: C. Hemoglobin A1c (HbA1c)
Reason: Hemoglobin A1c (HbA1c) is commonly used to monitor long-term blood sugar control in diabetic patients, as it reflects the average blood glucose levels over the past 2-3 months. Fasting plasma glucose (FPG), oral glucose tolerance test (OGTT), and random plasma glucose (RPG) are other tests used to diagnose or monitor diabetes, but HbA1c is the preferred test for long-term control assessment.

Answer: A. Statins
Reason: Statins are commonly used as a first-line treatment for hyperlipidemia, as they effectively lower low-density lipoprotein (LDL) cholesterol, the primary target in treating high cholesterol. Fibrates, niacin, and bile acid sequestrants may also be prescribed for cholesterol management, but statins are the preferred initial treatment.

Medical terminology

Answer: C. Difficulty breathing
Reason: Dyspnea is the medical term for Difficulty breathing or shortness of breath. This symptom can be associated with various respiratory and cardiovascular conditions, such as asthma, chronic obstructive pulmonary disease (COPD), and congestive heart failure.

Answer: B. Heart attack
Reason: Myocardial infarction (MI) is the medical term for a heart attack, which occurs when the blood supply to a part of the heart muscle is blocked, typically due to a blood clot. This can result in damage or death of the heart muscle cells, leading to the characteristic symptoms of chest pain, shortness of breath, and nausea, among others.

Answer: C. Stones
Reason: Nephrolithiasis is the medical term used to describe the presence of kidney stones, which are hard deposits of minerals and salts that form inside the kidneys. These stones can cause severe pain and other symptoms as they pass through the urinary tract.

Answer: A. Joint pain
Reason: Arthralgia is the medical term for joint pain, which various conditions, such as arthritis, injuries, or infections, can cause. The period does not specify the cause or severity of the joint pain, but it helps describe the symptom's location and nature.

Anatomy

Answer: A. Choroid plexus
Reason: The choroid plexus is a network of capillaries and specialized epithelial cells within the brain's ventricles. It produces cerebrospinal fluid (CSF), which provides cushioning and protection for the brain and spinal cord.

Answer: D. Reabsorb water and electrolytes
Reason: The primary function of the large intestine, also known as the colon, is to reabsorb water and electrolytes from the remaining indigestible food matter and to compact and eliminate the waste as feces. While some nutrient absorption occurs in the large intestine, the small intestine primarily absorbs most nutrients during digestion.

Answer: B. Two
Reason: The carpal bones of the human wrist are categorized into two rows: proximal and distal. Each row has four bones, with eight carpal bones in each wrist.

Answer: C. Iliopsoas
Reason: The iliopsoas muscle is a large, powerful muscle group composed of the iliacus and psoas major muscles. It is responsible for flexion and medial rotation of the hip joint. The iliopsoas muscle plays a significant role in walking, running, and maintaining an upright posture.

ICD-10-CM

Answer: A. I10
Reason: I10 is the ICD-10-CM code for essential (primary) hypertension, which is a condition characterized by persistently elevated blood pressure without an identifiable cause.

Answer: A. X
Reason: In ICD-10-CM, the character "X" is used as a placeholder for codes requiring a seventh character but not a sixth one. This ensures that the Code is formatted correctly and can be accurately processed.

Answer: C. E11.40
Reason: The ICD-10-CM code E11.40 represents type 2 diabetes mellitus with diabetic neuropathy, unspecified. Diabetic neuropathy is a type of nerve damage that can occur in patients with diabetes.

Answer: B. J20.6
Reason: J20.6 is the ICD-10-CM code for acute bronchitis due to the respiratory syncytial virus (RSV), a common virus that can cause respiratory infections, particularly in young children.

Answer: A. E11.331
Reason: The ICD-10-CM code E11.331 represents moderate, nonproliferative diabetic retinopathy without macular edema, in the right eye, due to type 2 diabetes mellitus. This Code specifies the severity of the retinopathy, the absence of macular edema, and the affected eye.

HCPCS Level II

Answer: A. G0008
Reason: HCPCS Level II code G0008 is used for reporting the administration of the seasonal influenza vaccine. This Code is specific to administering the flu vaccine and should not be confused with codes for other types of vaccinations.

Answer: D. K0001
Reason: The appropriate HCPCS Level II code for a standard manual wheelchair is K0001. This Code reports a wheelchair manually propelled by the patient or pushed by another individual.

Answer: A. J0585
Reason: HCPCS Level II code J0585 reports an injection of onabotulinumtoxinA (Botox) per unit. In this case, the Code would be written for ten units of Botox. The other codes listed (J0586, J0587, and J0588) represent different types of botulinum toxin injections, not onabotulinumtoxinA.

Coding Guidelines

Answer: C. Code both the acute and chronic conditions
Reason: ICD-10-CM coding guidelines instruct coders to code acute and chronic diseases when different codes are available, as both conditions are relevant to the patient's care.

Answer: B. The Code for the Encounter for Chemotherapy
Reason: When a patient is admitted to receive chemotherapy, the appropriate principal diagnosis code is the Code for the Encounter for chemotherapy, such as Z51.11.

Answer: C. Use the unilateral procedure code with a -50 modifier
Reason: According to CPT coding guidelines, when a procedure is performed bilaterally, the coder should use the unilateral procedure code with a -50 modifier to indicate that the process was performed on both sides of the body.

Answer: A. To indicate that two codes cannot be reported together
Reason: An Excludes1 note in ICD-10-CM indicates that two principles cannot be reported together because the conditions represented by the codes are mutually exclusive or cannot occur together.

Answer: A. Primary injury, secondary injury, external cause
Reason: According to ICD-10-CM coding guidelines, when coding for damages, the correct order for coding is primary injury, secondary injury, and external motivation.

Answer: B. Code all procedures and append modifier -51 to the secondary system (s)
Reason: Per CPT coding guidelines, when coding for multiple procedures performed during the same surgical session, the coder should code all procedures and append modifier -51 to the secondary system (s) to indicate that multiple procedures were performed.

Answer: B. Code the signs and symptoms related to the probable or suspected diagnosis
Reason: ICD-10-CM coding guidelines state that in an outpatient setting, if a diagnosis is documented as "probable" or "suspected," the coder should code the signs and symptoms related to the probable or suspected diagnosis rather than the diagnosis itself.
Compliance and Regulatory

Answer: B. Designating a compliance officer or contact
Reason: The OIG recommends that a medical practice designates a compliance officer or contact as a critical component of its compliance plan. This individual oversees and implements the practice's compliance program, ensuring the course adheres to relevant laws and regulations.

Answer: C. 30 days
Reason: According to HIPAA regulations, a covered entity must provide patients with access to their medical records within 30 days of the patient's request. The entity may extend this timeframe by 30 days if they provide a written explanation for the delay.

Answer: D. Routine wellness exams
Reason: The Stark Law specifically targets designated health services (DHS), which include physical therapy services, radiology services, and clinical laboratory services. Routine wellness exams are not considered DHS and are therefore not subject to the Stark Law.

Cases

1. **Solution:** The primary care physician should document the patient's symptoms, medical history, and examination findings and order diagnostic tests. The physician should also confirm the diagnosis, prescribed medication, dietary advice, and follow-up appointment information.

2. **Solution:** The surgeon should document the surgery, the postoperative infection, the prescribed antibiotics, and the follow-up appointment. The medical coder should use the appropriate ICD-10-CM and CPT codes to reflect the surgery, the postoperative infection, and the treatment provided.

3. **Solution:** The emergency department physician should document the patient's presenting symptoms, order tests, and diagnosis of myocardial infarction. The medical coder should use the appropriate ICD-10-CM and CPT codes to reflect the patient's condition, the tests ordered, and admission to the hospital.

4. **Solution:** The physician should document the well-child visit, including the patient's growth and development assessment, administered vaccinations, and the scheduled follow-up appointment. The medical coder should use the appropriate ICD-10-CM and CPT codes to reflect the well-child visit and vaccinations.

5. **Solution:** The dermatologist should document the suspicious skin lesion, the punch biopsy, and the pathology results. The medical coder should use the appropriate ICD-10-CM and CPT codes to reflect the patient's condition, the biopsy, and the pathology testing.

6. **Solution:** The surgeon should document the hernia repair surgery, the patient's discharge, and the postoperative care instructions. The medical coder should use the appropriate ICD-10-CM and CPT codes to reflect the surgery, the patient's release, and the prescribed medication.

7. **Solution:** The gastroenterologist should document the colonoscopy, the polyp removal, and the pathology results. The medical coder should use the appropriate ICD-10-CM and CPT codes to reflect the colonoscopy, the polyp removal, and the benign pathology results.

8. **Solution:** The psychiatrist should document the patient's symptoms, the evaluation, diagnoses, prescribed medication, and the scheduled follow-up appointment. The medical coder should use the appropriate ICD-10-CM and CPT codes to reflect the patient's conditions, the evaluation, and the prescribed medication.

9. **Solution:** The allergist should document the patient's symptoms, skin testing, and test results, prescribed allergy medication, and recommended immunotherapy. The medical coder should use the appropriate ICD-10-CM and CPT codes to reflect the patient's condition, the skin testing, and the prescribed medication.

10. **Solution:** The cardiologist should document the follow-up appointment, physical examination, stress test, and the results. The medical coder should use the appropriate ICD-10-CM and CPT codes to reflect the patient's previous myocardial infarction, the follow-up appointment, the stress test, and the continued treatment plan.

Ethical and Legal Considerations

1. **Answer: A.** Discussing a patient's medical condition with their family members without consent
   Reason: Patient confidentiality is a fundamental principle in healthcare, and sharing a patient's medical information without their consent is a violation of that principle. Options B, C, and D are all examples of appropriate actions that respect patient privacy and follow ethical guidelines.

2. **Answer: B.** To protect patient privacy and ensure the security of health information
   Reason: HIPAA was enacted to protect the privacy of patients' health information and ensure the security of electronic health records. The other options are not the main purposes of HIPAA.

3. **Answer: B.** Reporting only accurate and complete codes based on documentation
   Reason: Ethical coding practices involve reporting accurate and complete codes based on the medical documentation provided. The other options involve actions that could be considered fraudulent or unethical.

4. **Answer: B.** Ensuring accurate and compliant coding and billing practices
   Reason: Medical coders play a crucial role in preventing healthcare fraud and abuse by ensuring accurate and compliant coding and billing practices. While they may report unethical behavior, their primary role is not to investigate, advise patients, or report colleagues.

5. **Answer: A.** Respect the patient's autonomy and explore alternative treatment options
   Reason: Healthcare providers should respect a patient's autonomy and their right to make decisions about their own care, even if it means refusing a recommended treatment. They should work with the patient to explore alternative treatment options that align with the patient's beliefs and preferences.

6. **Answer: A.** A physician receives financial incentives for prescribing a specific medication
   Reason: A conflict of interest occurs when a healthcare provider's personal interests may compromise their professional judgment. Financial incentives for prescribing a specific medication could influence a physician's decision-making and lead to biased treatment recommendations.

7. **Answer: C.** To address healthcare fraud and abuse by penalizing the submission of false claims
   Reason: The False Claims Act is a federal law that addresses healthcare fraud and abuse by imposing penalties on individuals and organizations that submit false claims for reimbursement. The other options do not accurately describe the main purpose of the False Claims Act.

8. **Answer: D.** Major surgery
   Reason: Informed consent is a legal and ethical requirement for major medical interventions, such as surgery, to ensure that patients understand the risks, benefits, and alternatives before agreeing to the procedure. The other options typically do not require informed consent, as they are routine or less invasive interventions.

9. **Answer: A.** Report their concerns to a supervisor or compliance officer
   Reason: If a medical coder suspects fraudulent coding or billing practices in their workplace, the most appropriate action is to report their concerns to a supervisor or compliance officer who can investigate the issue further. The other options are not appropriate responses to suspected fraud.

10. **Answer: C.** To ensure that medical decisions are made in the best interest of patients
    Reason: The primary goal of medical ethics is to ensure that medical decisions are made in the best interest of patients, prioritizing their well-being, autonomy, and dignity. The other options do not accurately describe the primary goal of medical ethics.

Questions and Answers

QUESTION: What is the primary purpose of medical coding, and why is it essential in the healthcare industry?

ANSWER: The primary purpose of medical coding is to translate healthcare diagnoses, procedures, medical services, and equipment into universal medical alphanumeric codes. This standardized system is crucial for accurate documentation, billing, and reimbursement, as well as for statistical analysis, quality improvement, and compliance with regulations.

QUESTION: Explain the three main code sets used in medical coding and their respective applications.

ANSWER: The three main code sets are:

- ICD-10-CM (International Classification of Diseases, 10th Revision, Clinical Modification): Used to report diagnoses and medical conditions.
- CPT (Current Procedural Terminology): Used to report medical procedures and services performed by healthcare providers.
- HCPCS Level II (Healthcare Common Procedure Coding System): Reports supplies, equipment, and non-physician services, such as ambulance rides and durable medical equipment.

QUESTION: What is the role of a medical coder, and how does it differ from a medical biller?

ANSWER: A medical coder is responsible for accurately assigning codes to diagnoses, procedures, and services based on the patient's medical record. This process ensures proper documentation and reimbursement. On the other hand, a medical biller is responsible for submitting coded claims to insurance companies and managing the billing process. They follow up on claims, address denials, and work with patients to resolve payment issues.

QUESTION: What are the critical differences between ICD-10-CM and ICD-10-PCS, and when are they used?

ANSWER: ICD-10-CM (International Classification of Diseases, 10th Revision, Clinical Modification) reports diagnoses and medical conditions in all healthcare settings. It covers various diseases, injuries, and other health issues. ICD-10-PCS (International Classification of Diseases, 10th Revision, Procedure Coding System) reports hospital inpatient procedures. It provides a detailed classification system for surgical, diagnostic, and therapeutic strategies.

QUESTION: Explain the importance of modifiers in medical coding and provide an example of their use.

ANSWER: Modifiers are two-digit codes that provide additional information about a procedure or service, which can affect reimbursement. They help to clarify the specific circumstances under which a service was provided and ensure accurate billing. For example, modifier -59 (Distinct Procedural Service) can indicate that a separate, distinct service was performed during the same encounter, allowing for appropriate reimbursement for both services.

QUESTION: How do coding guidelines and conventions help ensure the accuracy and consistency of medical coding?

ANSWER: Coding guidelines and conventions provide standardized rules and instructions for using code sets. They help to ensure that medical coders apply codes correctly and consistently, promoting accurate documentation and billing. Adhering to these guidelines also helps to maintain compliance with regulatory requirements and reduce the risk of audits, denials, and penalties.

QUESTION: What are the primary responsibilities of a Certified Professional Coder (CPC)?

ANSWER: A Certified Professional Coder (CPC) is responsible for accurately assigning ICD-10-CM, CPT, and HCPCS codes to diagnoses, procedures, and services based on the patient's medical record. They must maintain up-to-date knowledge of coding guidelines, conventions, and payer-specific requirements. CPCs also ensured proper documentation, reimbursement, and regulation compliance.

QUESTION: What is the importance of medical terminology and anatomy knowledge for a medical coder?

ANSWER: Medical terminology and anatomy knowledge are essential for a medical coder to accurately interpret and code the information in a patient's medical record.

QUESTION: What are some common challenges medical coders face, and how can they overcome them?

ANSWER: Common challenges faced by medical coders include:

- Keeping up with frequent code set updates and changes in coding guidelines.
- Ensuring accurate and specific code assignment, particularly for complex or unusual cases.
- Meeting productivity and accuracy standards.
- Navigating payer-specific requirements and policies.
- To overcome these challenges, medical coders should engage in ongoing education, stay updated with industry news and changes, participate in coding forums or communities for peer support, and utilize coding resources and tools to improve efficiency and accuracy.

QUESTION: How do medical coders collaborate with other healthcare professionals to ensure accurate documentation and billing?

ANSWER: Medical coders work closely with healthcare providers, medical billers, and other revenue cycle team members to ensure accurate documentation and billing. They may seek clarification from providers regarding the documentation or medical necessity, educate providers on proper documentation practices, and collaborate with billers to address denials or payment discrepancies. Effective communication and teamwork are essential for maintaining a compliant and efficient revenue cycle process.

QUESTION: What is the purpose of an audit in medical coding, and what are some best practices for preparing for and responding to an audit?

ANSWER: An audit in medical coding is a systematic review of coded records to assess coding practices' accuracy, completeness, and compliance. Audits may be conducted internally or by external entities, such as insurance companies or regulatory agencies. Best practices for preparing for and responding to an audit include:

- Maintaining up-to-date knowledge of coding guidelines and payer-specific requirements.
- Implementing a comprehensive compliance plan and conducting regular internal audits.
- Ensuring clear and accurate documentation of coding rationale and decision-making.
- Addressing identified issues promptly and implementing corrective action plans as needed.

QUESTION: Describe the role of the Health Insurance Portability and Accountability Act (HIPAA) in medical coding and billing.

ANSWER: The Health Insurance Portability and Accountability Act (HIPAA) is a federal law that governs the privacy and security of protected health information (PHI). In medical coding and billing, HIPAA sets standards for electronic health information transmission, including standardized code sets and transaction formats. Medical coders and billers must adhere to HIPAA regulations to ensure PHI's confidentiality, integrity, and availability and avoid penalties for non-compliance.

QUESTION: What factors can influence the selection of the appropriate Evaluation and Management (E/M) code for a patient encounter?

ANSWER: The appropriate Evaluation and Management (E/M) code for a patient encounter is determined by considering factors such as:

- The type of service (e.g., new or established patient, consultation, preventive care).
- The setting where the service is provided (e.g., office, hospital, nursing facility).
- The complexity of the patient's medical history, examination, and decision-making.
- The amount of time spent by the provider on the encounter.
- Accurate E/M coding is essential for appropriate reimbursement and compliance with coding guidelines.

QUESTION: Explain the concept of medical necessity and its importance in medical coding and billing.

ANSWER: Medical necessity refers to the appropriateness and clinical justification of healthcare services, procedures, and treatments provided to a patient. It is a crucial factor in determining coverage and reimbursement by insurance companies. In medical coding and billing, medical necessity must be established and documented in the patient's medical record to support the codes assigned and the billed services. Failure to demonstrate a medical condition can result in claim denials, reduced reimbursement, or penalties for non-compliance.

QUESTION: What is the role of modifiers in medical coding, and how do they impact claim processing and reimbursement?

ANSWER: Modifiers are two-digit codes appended to CPT or HCPCS codes to provide additional information about the service or procedure performed. They help clarify the circumstances under which a service was provided and can impact claim processing and reimbursement. Modifiers may indicate that a service was distinct from others billed on the same day, performed on a different body part, or affected by a specific condition or situation. Using modifiers correctly ensures accurate billing and avoids claim denials or payment adjustments.

QUESTION: How do medical coders stay updated with coding guidelines, code sets, and payer-specific policies?

ANSWER: Medical coders can stay up-to-date with changes in coding guidelines, code sets, and payer-specific policies by:

- Participating in continuing education courses, webinars, or conferences.
- Subscribing to industry publications, newsletters, or email alerts.
- Following professional organizations, such as AAPC or AHIMA, on social media.
- Participating in coding forums, discussion boards, or local chapter meetings.
- Regularly reviewing updates from CMS, the AMA, or other authoritative sources.
- Staying current with industry changes is critical for maintaining coding accuracy and compliance.

QUESTION: What is the difference between facility and professional fee coding, and what factors should be considered when assigning codes in each setting?

ANSWER: Facility coding pertains to the assignment of codes for services provided in a hospital or other institutional setting, while professional fee coding focuses on services provided by individual healthcare providers, such as physicians or non-physician practitioners. In facility coding, coders must consider factors such as the resources used by the facility, the patient's clinical condition, and the complexity of the services provided. In professional fee coding, coders must consider the provider's documentation, the level of service offered, and the specific procedures or treatments performed. Understanding the differences between these settings is essential for accurate code assignment and appropriate reimbursement.

QUESTION: What are some best practices for preventing and addressing medical coding and billing claim denials?

ANSWER: Best practices for preventing and addressing claim denials in medical coding and billing include:

- Ensuring accurate and complete coding, including appropriate modifiers and diagnosis codes.
- Verifying patient eligibility and insurance coverage before rendering services.
- Staying current with payer-specific guidelines, policies, and requirements.
- Establishing a robust claim review and submission process to catch errors before submitting claims.
- Monitoring denial trends and implementing corrective action plans to address common issues.
- Providing ongoing education and training for coding and billing staff to improve accuracy and compliance.

QUESTION: Explain the importance of the National Correct Coding Initiative (NCCI) in medical coding and how it impacts claim processing and reimbursement.

ANSWER: The National Correct Coding Initiative (NCCI) is a CMS program that promotes correct coding practices and prevents improper payments for Medicare Part B claims. NCCI includes a set of coding edits, such as procedure-to-procedure (PTP) edits and medically unlikely amendments (MUEs), that identify potential coding errors or overpayments. Medical coders must be familiar with NCCI guidelines and adhere to them when assigning codes for services and procedures. Failure to follow NCCI guidelines can result in claim denials, reduced reimbursement, or penalties for non-compliance.

QUESTION: Describe the role of a compliance plan in medical coding and billing, and what elements should be included in an effective compliance plan?

ANSWER: A compliance plan is a set of policies and procedures to ensure that medical coding and billing practices adhere to relevant laws, regulations, and industry standards.

QUESTION: What is the difference between ICD-10-CM and ICD-10-PCS, and in which healthcare settings are they used?

ANSWER: ICD-10-CM (International Classification of Diseases, 10th Revision, Clinical Modification) is used to classify and report diagnoses in all healthcare settings. Healthcare providers use it to describe the patient's condition and the reason for their encounter. ICD-10-PCS (International Classification of Diseases, 10th Revision, Procedure Coding System) is used to classify and report inpatient procedures in hospital settings. While ICD-10-CM is used universally, ICD-10-PCS is specific to inpatient hospital procedures and is not used in outpatient or physician office settings.

QUESTION: How do medical coders ensure the accuracy of their coding and minimize the risk of errors or claim denials?

ANSWER: Medical coders can ensure the accuracy of their coding and minimize the risk of errors or claim denials by:

- Thoroughly reviewing the provider's documentation to identify all relevant diagnoses, procedures, and services.
- Staying current with coding guidelines, code updates, and payer-specific policies.
- Using appropriate coding resources, such as codebooks, coding software, and authoritative reference materials.
- Participating in ongoing education, training, and professional development opportunities.
- Seeking input or clarification from colleagues, supervisors, or providers when faced with complex or ambiguous coding scenarios.
- Regularly auditing and reviewing their work to identify and address any areas of weakness or potential risk.

QUESTION: What are the primary reasons for medical coding audits, and what benefits do they offer healthcare organizations?
ANSWER: Medical coding audits are performed to ensure coding practices' accuracy, completeness, and compliance. They help healthcare organizations identify and address potential issues, such as coding errors, documentation deficiencies, or non-compliance with coding guidelines and payer policies. Benefits of medical coding audits include:

- Improved coding accuracy and claim submission processes, leading to fewer claim denials and increased revenue.
- Enhanced compliance with laws, regulations, and industry standards, reducing the risk of penalties or sanctions.
- Identification of areas for education and training to improve coder performance and knowledge.
- Evaluation of the effectiveness of existing coding policies and procedures, allowing for adjustments and improvements as needed.

QUESTION: How does the HIPAA Privacy Rule impact medical coders and their access to protected health information (PHI)?
ANSWER: The HIPAA Privacy Rule establishes standards for protecting individuals' medical records and other personal health information. Medical coders are required to follow the HIPAA Privacy Rule when accessing, using, or disclosing PHI. This means that coders must limit their access to the minimum necessary information to perform their coding duties, safeguard PHI against unauthorized access or disclosure, and adhere to organizational policies and procedures for handling PHI. Failure to comply with the HIPAA Privacy Rule can result in penalties, sanctions, or other consequences for the coder and the organization.

QUESTION: What is the role of medical necessity in medical coding and billing, and how does it affect claim processing and reimbursement?
ANSWER: Medical necessity refers to the appropriateness and justification of a medical service or procedure based on a patient's condition and the standard of care. In medical coding and billing, medical necessity plays a crucial role in determining whether a service or procedure will be covered by the patient's insurance and reimbursed. Coders must ensure that the provider's documentation supports the benefits and practices they code and meet the criteria for medical necessity established by payers, such as Medicare or private insurance companies. Failure to demonstrate a medical condition can result in claim denials or reduced reimbursement.

QUESTION: What is the difference between modifier 59 and the X{EPSU} modifiers, and when should they be used in coding?
ANSWER: Modifier 59 (Distinct Procedural Service) and the X{EPSU} modifiers indicate that a service is separate and distinct from other services reported on the same claim. Modifier 59 is more general, while the X{EPSU} modifiers provide more specific information about the particular service. The X{EPSU} modifiers include:

- XE (Separate Encounter): Service was performed during a separate encounter.
- XP (Separate Practitioner): The service was performed by a different practitioner.
- XS (Separate Structure): Service was performed on a separate organ/structure.
- XU (Unusual Non-Overlapping Service): The service does not overlap the standard components of the primary benefit.

Coders should use modifier 59 or the appropriate X{EPSU} modifier when the documentation supports that a separate, distinct service was performed and when it is required by payer guidelines to bypass bundling edits or justify separate reimbursement.

QUESTION: How do medical coders stay current with changes to coding guidelines, code updates, and payer-specific policies?

ANSWER: Medical coders stay current with changes to coding guidelines, code updates, and payer-specific policies by engaging in the following activities:

- Regularly reviewing updates and announcements from coding organizations, such as the American Medical Association (AMA) or the Centers for Medicare and Medicaid Services (CMS).
- Attending coding conferences, webinars, workshops, or other educational events.
- Participating in coding-related forums, listservs, or social media groups.
- Subscribing to industry publications, newsletters, or alerts that provide updates on coding changes and guidelines.
- Engaging in ongoing professional development and pursuing relevant certifications or credentials.

QUESTION: What is the role of the National Correct Coding Initiative (NCCI) in medical coding and billing, and how do coders use the NCCI edits to ensure accurate coding?

ANSWER: The National Correct Coding Initiative (NCCI) is a CMS program to promote accurate coding and prevent improper payment for Medicare Part B claims. The NCCI establishes a set of coding edits, known as NCCI edits, that identify code pairs that should not be billed together under specific circumstances. Coders use the NCCI edits to ensure accurate coding by reviewing the amendments and applying them to claims before submission. If the coder identifies an improvement that affects their share, they must either modify the declaration to comply with the edit or provide documentation to support an exception, such as appending an appropriate modifier. Failure to follow the NCCI edits can result in claim denials or payment reductions.

QUESTION: How do medical coders determine the correct level of Evaluation and Management (E/M) service to code for a patient encounter?

ANSWER: Medical coders determine the correct level of E/M service to code for a patient encounter by reviewing the provider's documentation and considering the following components: history, examination, and medical decision-making. The coder must evaluate the extent and complexity of each element documented in the medical record and compare it to the guidelines established by the AMA or CMS. Additionally, coders must consider factors such as the type of encounter (e.g., new or established patient), the setting (e.g., office, hospital), and any relevant modifiers. The coder selects the E/M code that best represents the level of service provided based on the documentation and the applicable guidelines.

QUESTION: What is the role of diagnosis codes in medical billing, and how do they impact claim processing and reimbursement?

ANSWER: Diagnosis codes are used in medical billing to describe the patient's condition and the reason for the encounter or service. They are crucial for claim processing and reimbursement because they help establish the medical necessity of the services provided. Payers use diagnosis codes to determine coverage, reimbursement rates, and claim payment. Accurate and specific diagnosis coding can result in timely claim processing and the appropriate fee, while incorrect or vague diagnosis codes may lead to claim denials or payment delays.

QUESTION: What is the difference between a primary and secondary diagnosis, and how do coders determine which diagnosis to list first on a claim?

ANSWER: A primary diagnosis is the main reason for a patient's encounter with a healthcare provider, while secondary diagnoses are additional conditions that coexist with the primary diagnosis or that impact the patient's care. Coders determine which diagnosis to list on a claim by reviewing the provider's documentation and identifying the condition that is chiefly responsible for the services provided. The primary diagnosis should be listed first on the share, followed by any secondary diagnoses in order of significance to the patient's care.

QUESTION: How do coders handle incomplete or unclear documentation when assigning codes?
ANSWER: When coders encounter incomplete or unclear documentation, they should follow a query process to seek clarification from the provider. The coder should only make assumptions or assign codes based on their interpretation of the documentation with confirmation from the provider. A query can be written or verbal, but written questions are generally preferred as they create a documented record of the communication between the coder and the provider. Maintaining an open line of communication between coders and providers is essential to ensure accurate and complete coding, which ultimately supports appropriate reimbursement and quality patient care.

QUESTION: What is the role of the medical coder in the revenue cycle, and how does accurate coding contribute to a healthcare organization's financial health?
ANSWER: The medical coder plays a critical role in the revenue cycle by translating clinical documentation into standardized codes that can be used for billing, reporting, and analysis. Accurate coding is essential for a healthcare organization's financial health, directly impacting claim reimbursement and compliance with payer policies and regulations. Proper coding can reduce claim denials, improve cash flow, and minimize the risk of audits and penalties. Additionally, accurate coding contributes to the overall data quality, supporting decision-making, quality improvement initiatives, and population health management efforts.

QUESTION: What are the critical steps in the coding process, from receiving the medical record to submitting the coded claim?
ANSWER: The critical steps in the coding process include:

- Receiving the medical record: Coders obtain the medical record, either in paper or electronic format, from the healthcare provider or facility.
- Reviewing the documentation: Coders carefully review the clinical documentation to identify all services, procedures, and diagnoses that need to be coded.
- Assigning codes: Coders give the appropriate codes based on the documentation and applicable coding guidelines, selecting the most specific codes available.
- Validating the codes: Coders verify the accuracy of the assigned codes by cross-checking them with the documentation and relevant coding resources, such as codebooks, guidelines, or payer policies.
- Preparing the claim: Coders enter the assigned codes into the claim form or billing software, ensuring all required information is complete and accurate.
- Submitting the coded claim: The coded claim is submitted to the payer electronically or via paper submission for processing and payment.

CONCLUSION

As a result, the CPC Test Guide is a comprehensive and priceless tool for aspiring medical coders who want to pass the Certified Professional Coder (CPC) exam. Anesthesia, radiology, laboratory/pathology, medicine, medical terminology, anatomy, ICD-10-CM, HCPCS, compliance and regulatory issues, ethical and legal considerations, and many other essential topics are covered in the guide. The guide contains many examples, case studies, and multiple-choice questions to aid test-takers in comprehending and applying the concepts.

Medical coding is constantly developing with changes to regulatory standards, upgrades to coding systems, and improvements in healthcare technology. As a result, it's critical for aspiring programmers to stay current with market trends and to keep a solid grounding in coding fundamentals and best practices. This manual intends to provide CPC applicants with the knowledge and abilities required to succeed in their chosen field, ensuring a smooth entry into the medical coding industry.

Test-takers who learn the information in this manual will not only be well-prepared for the CPC examination but will also be better able to deal with the difficulties of a career in medical coding. It is impossible to emphasize the significance of accurate coding in the current healthcare environment because it directly impacts patient care, provider reimbursement, and the overall quality of healthcare data. Medical coders are essential to the revenue cycle, and the financial stability of healthcare institutions dramatically benefits from their knowledge.

From the initial phases of preparation for the CPC examination to continuing to advance their abilities and knowledge throughout their careers, the CPC Test Guide is an invaluable resource in supporting the professional development of medical coders. The manual's focus on practical applications and real-world examples guarantees that readers can immediately apply the information to their everyday work, building a deeper understanding of the subject and supporting professional development.

The CPC Test Guide's overarching objective is to encourage accurate coding, compliance, and high-quality patient care throughout the healthcare profession by assisting coders in obtaining certification and excelling in their jobs. Instilling confidence and competence in their talents as they strive towards CPC certification and a lucrative career in medical coding, the handbook equips aspiring coders to take the next step in their professional journey by offering a thorough, accessible, and exciting resource.

SPECIAL BONUS

D ear reader, I would be grateful if you would take a minute of your time and post a review on AMAZON to let other users know how this experience was and what you liked most about the book. Also, I have recently decided to give a **gift** to all our readers. Yes, I want to provide you with the assistance that will help you with your study you will receive

- **Audiobook (mp3 audio files)** from listening to whenever and wherever you want!
- **This book in digital format**
- **BOOK 1: "Medical Billing & Coding 2023-2024 Study Guide".**
- **BOOK 2: "Medical Terminology". NOTE.** This book has also been made into **400 digital flashcards,** and you can use it to repeat and memorize.
- **50 Digital Flashcards with practical examples** of how these terms are used in medical billing and coding practice. Each flashcard describes a different pathology or medical condition, with a unique case illustrating how that manifests itself and how it can be treated. Thus, you will have a wide range of knowledge and be able to apply it to different clinical situations.

You can track your progress and conveniently and interactively memorize the most important terms and concepts! Download to your device: **Anki APP or AnkiDroid**, or enter the web page and register free of charge. Then import the files we have given you as a gift and use the flashcards whenever and wherever you want to study and track your progress.

Below you will find a QR CODE that will give you direct access to this bonus (file to download directly to your device) without having to subscribe to any mailing list or leave your personal information.

I hope you will appreciate it.

To communicate with us directly, please write to us at
info.testbookreader@gmail.com

We are waiting for your feedback on amazon, in any case!
A cordial greeting; we wish you all the best.

Thank you!

THANK YOU!

Made in the USA
Las Vegas, NV
05 August 2023

7570574BR00050